ARCHITECTURE
of the
NOVEL

OTHER BOOKS BY JANE VANDENBURGH

A Pocket History of Sex
in the Twentieth Century: A Memoir

The Physics of Sunset: A Novel

Failure to Zigzag: A Novel

ARCHITECTURE

of the

NOVEL

a writer's handbook

PLOT, STORY, AND THE MECHANICS
OF NARRATIVE TIME

Carmichael Reid

Jane Vandenburgh

foreword by Anne Lamott

COUNTERPOINT

BERKELEY

Library of Congress Cataloging-in-Publication Data

Vandenburgh, Jane.
Architecture of the novel : a writer's handbook / by Jane Vandenburgh ;
foreword by Anne Lamott.
p. cm.
ISBN-13: 978-1-58243-597-8
ISBN-10: 1-58243-597-9
1. Fiction—Authorship—Handbooks, manuals, etc. 2. Fiction—Technique—
Handbooks, manuals, etc. I. Title.

PN3365.V25 2010
808.3—dc22

2010016791

Cover design by Natalya Balnova
Interior design by Megan Jones Design
Printed in the United States of America

COUNTERPOINT
1919 Fifth Street
Berkeley, CA 94710
www.counterpointpress.com
Distributed by Publishers Group West

10 9 8 7 6 5 4 3 2 1

The order of your book must proceed on this plan:
first simple beams, then those supported from below,
then suspended in part, then wholly suspended.
Then beams supporting other weights.

—LEONARDO DA VINCI, *THE NOTEBOOKS,* 1452

CONTENTS

ARCHITECTURE
of the
NOVEL

FOREWORD

BY ANNE LAMOTT

*A*RCHITECTURE OF THE NOVEL is a book after my own heart, rich in paradoxes and yet wonderfully plain, with an insistence on structure and discipline. It is also a call to freedom. It's about how to write a novel, why you *must* write a novel, and why the time is now.

As with everything Jane Vandenburgh has written, I'm amazed by her generous and ferocious mind, by the way she is able to edify and encourage and entertain, all on the same page. I'm not sure who else could write about the mysteries of how we tell our stories with such vigor and intelligence, curiosity and insight. Her ability to clarify the wheres and hows of writing fiction, her instructions on where to begin, on how to listen as the story and its characters reveal themselves to us, how to soar as a novelist while keeping things simple and real, almost make me want to write another novel.

Because it is *really* hard, and it takes such rigorous commitment! Any writer who tells you differently is either lying or has missed the boat. But *Architecture of the Novel* reminds me of all the good news, too, that the story already exists inside us, that telling the story is worth it.

In her own novels, Jane Vandenburgh has written about life and people with directness and lyricism and hard-won humor. In her ability to articulate the great themes of our lives and literature, of time and loss, love and resurrection, she can be exhilarating, scary, calming and intense, all at once. Her mind and heart are those of a poet, but her passion has always been the narrative in its longer form.

How do we tap into our own sensitivity, our own wildness of spirit, while structuring our moments and scenes into something coherent, tangible, cohesive, something that can be held—as she puts it—like a glass of clear water. Here you find the words of someone who has been sharing these secrets for a long time, of how to create a narrative, how to discover and be true to our characters, how to tough it out when it gets hard. She knows how easy it is to give up, how difficult it sometimes is to find your own voice, how necessary bad writing is, how bad writing leads to better writing if only you will let it, maybe even something close to what we had in mind all along. She knows a lot about truth and survival and the brokenness we all share, and man, she knows a lot about *writing*.

All of her books, and this one in particular, remind me of physical things I love. One is a nearby boulder that I visit fairly often, at American Soil in Marin County where I live—this rock is everything wonderful and grave and heavy and weightless and lovely all at once.

It weighs in at over a ton and it is the platonic essence of ROCK, slate gray and brown and craggy, but also curvaceous and ribboned with broad streams of rose quartz, which is all about love. It is tiled with moss green lichen, soft as fur or feathers, and on its top floor—the penthouse of this rock—are all sorts of little caverns and cavities and cracks and openings that create ponds of water, and gardens that hold tiny curly richly alive and brilliant green plants and shoots; and if you are the kind of person willing to pay attention, you'll meet teeny little creatures, hilarious and heartbreaking. You could stare at it and listen to it for hours, and you'll want to hold it, and share it with everyone you know.

This book in your hands contains what you need to get your novel written—and to discover the truth of who you are. It sort of tricks you into insisting on telling the truth, with your own voice and experiences and rhythms, even though if you are anything like me, her writing always makes me want to sound more like her. Her heart is strong and it is equally soft, as is yours. She is exotic and plain and down to earth, like you and maybe most of your favorite writers, and she shows you in this book how you can access and hone the gift of successfully telling the story that is yours alone to create.

Jane is brilliant, lovely, difficult, dark, aglow, and dangerous, rascally and sad, hilarious, spontaneous and talkative, with deep curiosity and lots of attitude. She might and almost certainly will say anything that crosses her mind. Maybe you have always dreamt that one day you, too, might capture your own version of this, on paper, both to help you figure out what your version even is, and in order to give it away.

That day is now, and I present a blueprint of how to make that happen. But be careful. This book is going to ruin your excuses, and your tendency to procrastinate. It's going to make it possible for you to redeem earlier senses of failure and you from your foolishness in thinking you could ever become a novelist.

And the second physical thing *Architecture* reminds me of is my favorite album from thirty . . . plus . . . years ago, when I was a very young writer. The record was called *Eat a Peach*, by the Allman Brothers, recorded live at the Fillmore East. There's a thirty-three-minute jam session with Gregg Allman, Dickey Betts, Berry Oakley, Butch Trucks, Jai Johanson; but mostly it's the last recorded slide guitar by late and very great Duane Allman, who died before the album was even issued. This one track took the Donovan Leitch song "There Is a Mountain," which goes, "First there is a mountain, then there is no mountain . . . then there is," which, if you think about it, pretty much says it all, and these guys played it with such aching greatness and passion (and maybe stonedness) and confidence and edge and sexuality that it was almost devastating—but instead it's one of the most beautiful rock and blues pieces in history. And it all springs from a simple tune, something you might sing to a child.

After establishing the melody—and *only* because of its careful establishment—Duane Allman started playing passages that took you so far out there that you couldn't imagine how he could possibly bring you back home. But because of the clarity of his guitar's voice, you heard something right away that had a crystalline energy to it, the ring of truth, that is really all that ever totally hooks us. As with a novel you love, you *had* to keep listening to it, had to keep turning the pages. And because you hung in there, and because he stayed so true to what was in his heart and mind, the song took you to the moon, and to the inner reaches of the human experience, and it made you want to cry and dance and shout, and it made you kind of crazy, in the freedom way, even as it somehow comforted you. Then it slowly, luxuriously, brought you back home. Only of course you weren't the same person you'd been before you'd taken the journey, or you were, but maybe more so, and which is the greatness of art.

I wouldn't read this book unless you are serious about wanting to try and do that, too, to find your way through the stories within, listening for the melody, trusting in the structure while finding your wings, and living the life of a writer.

PART ONE

*Longer discussions of terms appearing
in italic in Part One may appear in Part Two,
the alphabetical expanded glossary.*

1

Getting Started: Stop the Car!

THE JOKE IN my family is that on any car ride through even the most implausible town or countryside, I've always felt the need to stop the car. *Stop the car!* I'd yell. *I have to go to the bathroom!*

True enough, though the need was more basic: Ever since I was a little girl, I've been overwhelmed by the urge to get out and walk around, to be able to stand on this ground, breathe in this air, and speak to some living soul who inhabits *this specific place.*

Stop the car! I'd say, overwhelmed by my desire to hear and feel myself, to be set down *exactly* in another temporal location, some time and place that always felt more vivid and alive than my own reality. I'd need to hear, for instance, natives saying the name of the place I call *Baltimore* but they call *Ball-a-mer.*

(What I really needed, of course, was the experience all good books offer, as I found out later after I'd started reading them.)

Stop the car! might happen no matter where I'd find myself, in even the most wretched, run-down, rust-belt-ish sort of place, the abandoned train station on the wrong side of the new and gleaming sports arena, where the need to *Stop the car!* became especially urgent because I'd have noticed the sign in the window of some low-life dive that reads OUR BURGERS ARE NEVER SERVED WITH LETTUCE AND TOMATO!

Or it'll be *Stop the car! Let's get drinks at that bodega!*—and it's not the diet soda I want so much as the bodily sensations, the smells, the feel of the air against my skin, the quality of the dusty light that will, forever after, give this place back to me, so well remembered that it feels gift-wrapped.

I'm like a sensory shoplifter who grabs up one of the weekly throwaways from their stack in the corner of this crowded neighborhood groceria, the crumpled shopper that already looks so much like trash that I must jam it down into my book bag to hide it from my Loved Ones. They've spotted my inordinate attachment to what must seem like random stuff, these seemingly worthless things—sights, sounds, smells, impressions—all of which identify me as one of the *noticers*.

But these items are not worthless, nor are they random. They are, in fact, my gold, my silver, fragments that will, later on, begin to pulse with meaning, as if they have entire worlds packed down into them, worlds wanting to blaze outward from that initiating coal, illuminating their realities scene by vivid scene.

Back home, I'll get the shopper out, smooth it in my lap, flip to the classifieds to read the help-wanteds, the rentals, the Lost, the Found, the pets for sale, spotting the Chihuahua mix I'm evidently adopting, since I've already named it Diego.

Train station. Dive bar. Bodega. Diego: linguistic artifacts, each becoming the crystal that will, when encouraged, begin to self-elaborate, the chunk of granite from which I'll grow my own novelistic Sierra Madre.

⇒

THAT I AM a natural storyteller can be readily told by the way I resist the norm of beginning with an Author's Preface and slip instead into the galloping rhythms of exploration, my needing to *Stop the car!* so we can follow the thread of the tale down any half-promising byway. The narrative is—has always been—the place where I seek refuge.

But storytelling comes no more naturally to me than it does to you. We have a shared affinity deriving from our need to make coherent sense of what we come across in our everyday lives, this being what makes us human.

The biggest difference between you and me is that I've been a writer for so long that I'm now well attuned to my own witching stick. I know when my narrative divining rod has taken over and has climbed into the driver's seat, and is now swerving, braking, parking, dragging me from behind the wheel. I can see that its tip is pointing *exactly* at what it needs me to see, the narrative object that wants to be held to the light—so I can notice the way it's shining out in all its novelistic possibilities.

It is through practice that writers come by this sure sense of what will begin to feel like *recognition*. We seem to *encounter* our characters—their speech, their looks, their complex and interesting situations—instead of *inventing* them: The good-time girl living upstairs from the bodega already has her own story, and this entire story comes to us expressing an entire world of narrative context.

Her name is Gigi—she uses stars, not dots, in the *i*'s of her name, as I saw when I read it etched into the stall of the groceteria's restroom. All of us recognize the cadences of this kind of obviously made-up name, too spangled and gaudy to be real, a name Gigi took when her life began to veer off and go even more seriously wrong. It went wrong, then wrong again; we all know how the angle of her narrative divining rod tipped and pointed at the place where her boyfriend slipped out at dawn and got on the train.

Writers of fiction simply know these things. We're both cursed and blessed by the witching stick, by three weird sisters who crouch together over the pot of narrative, whispering as they concoct the future, making it up out of a pinch of this and a pound of that. For us they are indispensable, these fairy god witches of ours, whose names are Plot, Story, and the Mechanics of Narrative Time, in that we won't be able to write a good book without them. We rely upon them, those of us working to write in the longer narrative forms.

Briefly, it goes like this: Plot and story are opposite yet integral sides of the same one thing. A novel is like a glass of water, its story being the H_2O as liquid that fills the glass, just as plot is the glass itself, that which gives the water its size and shape and dimension.

The mechanics of the narrative time, meanwhile, give us the Laws of Nature of the world we are creating. These are very basic and include how gravity works in this place, as well as the other rules of physics. These natural laws will be uniform and will govern all matter and energy in a coherent way, so the physical world of this universe seems plausible.

The mechanics of narrative time make certain that all parts of the novel hang together and remain coherently united, that the glass set down upon the counter stays where it's been put, placed on the surface of the counter until some force comes along to lift it and carry it, to place it somewhere else. The physics of our narrative say that water poured into this glass stays inside this glass, instead of tumbling upward, flinging itself outward like shining drops of mercury floating into space.

Without something to contain it and the narrative mechanics to hold it down, your story will spill outward, upward, and away from you. Without a living, sloshing, moving, changing *something* active in the glass, your plot remains an empty vessel.

➤

ALL THIS PERTAINS because your novel wants nothing more than to convince us that it really is *like life*. As you write your novel, and then rewrite it, it will become a better and better book as it moves in the direction of this conviction. A fictional narrative wants to feel as if it hasn't been invented, as if it has, in fact, pre-existed in another realm and that what you've done is gone out to discover it. This means that you and I don't need to create the world in which the story is playing out as much get in the car and let the witching rod direct us to where we want to go.

We write to find ourselves in that specific time and place where the need to *Stop the car!* becomes all but overwhelming, where you see your novel's characters and settings and activities there before your eyes, alive and happening, seemingly of their own accord.

This is true no matter which variety or realm of Truth your novel works to occupy, whether its derives from autobiographical impulse or takes place Off-Gravity, in another virtual world inhabited by bright blue, flat-nosed avatars who will still be strangely familiar.

Regardless of the world in which they're placed, the rules for narrative remain remarkably the same. Our stories are informed by our own experiences as living, breathing, thinking, feeling individuals who are wide awake and are noticing these all-important details—and by our using what we notice to reach out to our readers, so that they, too, are able to live this story, from the other side of the page.

The means by which we make these connections are the immortal bonds, the same ones that have operated in storytelling from the beginning of time. There are three of them: *sympathy*, *empathy*, and a *correlation to our intuition about reality*. We learned these so long ago that they feel entirely natural to us. These are the same tools the novelist in every genre must and will employ.

⇒

SO YOU ARE, in fact, already well equipped to write a book from a lifetime of reading books, and because the structure of the longer narrative is one that mimics the rhythms of nature.

Still, writing an entire book seems like one of the more ambitious things for a person to want to do. You add to this a basic fact that makes it seem impossible: Frankly, you don't know how.

You don't know how because you don't yet know your novel's structure. You'd like to be given clear and firm directions, but you also know that one size, in this endeavor, will not fit all.

One size does not fit all, and the world you want to make is unlike any other, which means the only person who can write the book you don't yet know how to write is *you*.

This is why it's tough: Structure of the longer narrative is necessarily hard, in that no step-by-step directions exist that will tell you how you're going to go about writing the one book you need to write. The blueprints and materials list don't exist, and they won't until that time when you, yourself, can make them.

This is the terrible truth about the book you want to write: The only one who understands what all this entails is you. And the only way you're going to discover what this is, is by writing it.

This sounds like the Kevin Costner movie about ghosts and baseball heroes whose catchphrase was "If you build it, he will come." It sounds like the National Museum of the American Indian, on the Mall in Washington, D.C., built as if there were neither blueprints nor right angles and had to, in fact, be built once to teach its builders how to build it, correctly, again. All a little too woo-woo and mystical for those of us who prefer our directions numbered and set out in order. So far, little that you've read here about the construction of the longer narrative may sound helpful.

This is the reason that all of the other how-to books will programmatically fail you: The rules regarding the construction of our books are, of necessity, wrong for you because your book is individual. This means only *your novel itself* can tell you exactly how it needs to be made. No one aside from you, your book's writer, has ever existed within the narrative spaces of this story. No one else has seen what there is to see, heard what there is to hear, there in your story's rooms where your story is already hanging out.

This is the truth about novelistic structure: Every novel is both unique and self-devised. A novel's plot and structure—the glass that holds the living, sloshing, gushing, bubbling water—exist for exactly that one reason, which is to be exactly the right size and shape and form to hold the one narrative it is being made to contain, that is, your novel and no one else's.

What this means is that a narrative design emerges in one way only, and this is in tandem with its use. We call this its *architecture*, in which structure is shaped to fit exactly its purpose and its use. To the degree this architecture is successful, we find the shape and its narrative beautiful.

This may seem hard because it sounds circular in its logic, as if you're being asked to use your hand to draw the picture of the hand holding the pencil that's drawing the hand holding the pencil.

If you've been trying to write a novel and have so far failed, it may be because you haven't yet settled down and become comfortable with the build-it-and-he-will-come, chicken-and-egg dynamic.

A novel has mystical, self-generative properties—it wants to prove itself to you if you can relax and let it.

⮑

YOUR NOVEL — THE ONE that *you yourself* have been wanting to write—has all of these many elements that only you can know. Since you haven't actually had a chance to write it yet, these elements remain hidden from even you.

The irony is, of course, that the only way for you to discover what your novel holds is for you to trust yourself and your book enough to go ahead and write it. "OK, I will," you say. "I'll go ahead and write it as soon as someone tells me what its structure is," though this is exactly what no one can yet possibly know.

And this is the reason we have to give ourselves over to this task with a sense of courage and adventure, as if we're going off to discover a continent for which maps don't exist, because it is so far unexplored.

In design we follow the precept that Form Follows Function, which says that the architecture of your novel is a discovery you will come to. And because this discovery rushes to meet you at the moment of your need, you may well be astonished by the degree to which all of this becomes orderly and intentional, as if corresponding to some Higher Intelligence.

You trust yourself by putting gas in the car and heading out across the countryside, allowing the divining rod of the narrative itself to point you in the direction you need to go.

WHAT MAKES THIS work difficult is also what makes it so magical and rewarding: The architecture of your novel will be unique and original, and in it, form will follow function so that plot and story will entirely match.

You cannot yet know what shape your plot will take because you don't yet know its story. It is said that there are only three or four stories, that this handful of stories that exist keep repeating and repeating themselves as forcefully as if they had no idea they'd ever been told before.

There may be only a couple of stories, but there are also many intricate, very personally devised variations on these tales, as many versions as there are storytellers, as many perspectives on these stories as there are points of view.

Our stories are so human, so much a part of who we are, that they grow and change and evolve. Stories are adaptive, fitting into the times and places in which they find themselves, always learning the newest idiom in which to be expressed. The narrative power we admire in a good story is something the story comes by naturally.

All that we—our stories' writers—need to learn to do is trust them to go where they need to go.

➤

SO MANY OF us feel like we have this huge big story lying only half asleep within us, waiting only for the moment we have the time and silence and space and money and peace of mind that will finally allow us to sit down and listen to what this story has to say. All that we need—we feel—is to become attentive enough to our story for it to begin to tell itself to us. It does seem to exist almost preternaturally, as if it has come from where it already seems to exist, in hibernation.

The silence we feel we need will happen—we seem to think—in a little while: as soon as we get out of school or when the kids are older or when we can carve out some vacation time, or when this, that, or the other happens.

We can write our novel, we think, as soon as we retire.

Putting it off keeps us from the dread of that moment when we sit down and stare at the pulsing screen of the laptop or at the proverbial sheet of bright white paper, each shimmering in its emptiness. Here we are, but our story lies elsewhere, off in some darker place, an unclaimed continent, accessible only in our half-remembered dreams.

➤

WE TRUST FORM to follow function. We trust that we can learn the whole by creating the smallest of its parts. The structure of the novel we want to write may become as elaborate as the Victoria and Albert Museum, but we can't begin by trying to imagine that, as the act of even trying to imagine something so huge and so complex is immediately defeating.

Instead we trust the divining rod of the story itself, figuring that it will guide us, following it moment by moment into the yet-to-be-discovered continent. When we come we'll discover that we've already built it.

It's a Zen koan: We build a structure by paying structure no mind at all. We act as if this structure already exists, which—according to the rules of story—it already does. A narrative is made by creating the sense of action that has come to life within the temporal rooms of the structure it invents by the fact that action is taking place inside of it.

⇒

IN ORDER TO write a novel, all you must do is break the story down into its most fundamental parts. You write a scene. A *scene*—also called an *episode*—is the most fundamental element of narrative structure, a novel's most basic building block.

A scene is simple and easy to understand: At a certain time and in a specific place, an action has been allowed to happen, an action that plays out before the witness of our senses.

The novel is long and complex and can be hard to write, but the scene is simple. This is why we start there and why—whenever we get confused—we retreat to this most basic of narrative tasks: You write one scene and then you write another one.

A scene or episode contains a narrative incident or event. All this means is that *something happens*. No one needs to tell us anything about whatever it is that's happening—that is, this event or incident requires no preamble or explanation. It happens before the witness of our senses in a manner vivid enough that we feel we've entered the bodega and can experience it. Something's happened. Because of this, something else is just about to happen.

Everyone can write an episode. It is simply that: a segment of living time that contains dramatic action. An episode shows this action rather than laboriously telling us all about it:

"Stop the car!" she said, but the rest of them were laughing and talking and the volume on the radio was pumped up, so no one was paying attention.

"I mean it," she said. "There's something going on in there. Pull in, park right there, next to the beer truck. Come on, just do it!"

The car crunched across the gravel, hadn't even come to a complete stop before the girl threw the door open and got out, sprinting the fifteen feet to the half-open door of the bodega.

The bell sounded as she pulled the door open. "*Hola!*" she called, yelling it back into the shadows. "Is anybody here?" she yelled. "Gigi! I've come to get Diego."

This is a scene or episode in which the action is being *shown* to us directly rather than *summarized*. In action that is summarized, we feel time to be encapsulated as having already transpired, its actions finished, its possibilities shut down. Writing scenes in summary tells the reader that nothing exciting enough happened in this scene for us to bother witnessing it.

Writing in episode allows a scene to play out dramatically, so it asks that the events that are shown be meaningful to the storyline. When you're writing scenes that happen along the line of the story, they automatically lead to another scene, each asking, *And then . . . ?*

This is the way good books are *always* written: You write an episode, then you write another one. You do not worry about structuring the narrative whole because that whole can be made only by working from the inside out.

This is form following function, the novel's storytelling being its function and its form being the plot. We never know where we are going until we get there.

So let's get started.

2

Story

THE MOMENT WE begin to operate in the vicinity of our stories, we start to feel the pressure of their welling up in us, as if they sense our interest and have started migrating toward the crack that will lead them upward and out of darkness.

It is exactly this urgency—our stories saying they *really need to get started*—that we'll soon begin to depend upon.

But this same impulse would also have us rushing off to start without knowing much about what we think we're doing, which is what's gotten us into trouble in the past. For this reason we need to take a minute to articulate not only what may go wrong, but also what actually does need to happen.

What so frequently goes on, as we sit down, is that we feel the monumental nature of the undertaking and it occurs to us that *we're trying to write a novel*! This has the immediate effect of sending us searching for what will sound to our ear like novel-istic language, and—before we know it—we're writing *as if* we're writing a novel instead of doing the more important thing, merely allowing a story to be told.

The reason's simple: We prefer sounding as if we know what we're doing, so we naturally try to fabricate something overarching and thematic, our own version of *It was the best of times, it was the worst of times.*

We all have the sound of magnificent novels in our mind's ear—it's natural to want to write like this. We think we need to be creating beautiful language instead of creating *scenes*, when the vivid specificity of scenes is the only place the story actually exists.

Then, too, we sometimes will fall in love with this gorgeous language that we've worked so hard at writing, and we're sud-denly lost in a world of confusion.

What we've almost always done is to start out by writing *about* what our novel maybe thinks it might want to be about, as soon as it gets going. We're also usually trying to write *well*, to write *memorably*, one of the major impediments to anyone who's trying to get a novel going.

I myself have produced literally thousands of pages of this kind of novelistic-sounding language, all of it OK, or even good, or even *really very* good. Its main problem? The story is either buried under a crush of this self-bedazzled language or has gone completely missing.

At this earliest of stages we need to concentrate on the actual modesty of the task at hand, which is that we care *only about the story* and that our story doesn't really *care* about what good writers we may think we are.

Your story, in fact, actively dislikes self-important-sounding writing, because it works against every story's chief narrative ambition: to evaporate all sense of words on the page. Your story actually resents that it requires written language in order to tell itself, because it wants to be *believed in*, as story—that is, taken up *as reality* in the listener's mind. It doesn't want to dress up and go flouncing around as *art*.

Instead, your story would like us to hush up and simply follow it down into the place in narrative time where things seem to be already *happening*—as incidents and events unfolding before our eyes and ears, where everything is sensory and immediate, where our story's scenes are allowed to enact themselves before the witness of our senses.

The narrative mechanism that we call story runs along a fast, flat track in one linear direction. A story moves always and inevitably from the Now of the scene at hand forward in the direction of its own narrative future. The story asks only to have its events set out *in scene* in their narrative time and place. Story's nature is scant, simple, direct, and always, always active.

We start with story not only because it's the easiest place to start—it's also the most necessary. Story is most simply defined as a procession of meaningful events: those actions that take place along the *storyline* and serve to move narrative through to its conclusion. We do not observe the story from on high or make comments on these events from far, far away.

Story consists of events taking place *in scene*. The king dies. The queen dies. We want to witness these events.

The king dies. The queen dies. That's it: We amass scenes that show the story's events and incidents. This is all we need to do at first. We write our story's action.

And a story admits no pauses, no twists and leaps of well-plotted logic, no flights off the storyline and into eloquence, no moments where language turns around and begins to talk about itself.

A story says *This happens, this happens.* It conducts itself always by the simple act of allowing its scenes to enact themselves dramatically, by showing their incidents and events. Since a story doesn't want us to become overly aware of the language with which it's being written, it will try to tell itself directly, in the most plain way, using the kind of neutral wording that allows its writer little or nothing by way of interpretation.

Most stories want neither to be written in nor discussed in the third person. They will not have you or me looking down on them, talking over their heads, explaining aloud what's going on within them. Story takes place independently of all commentary. Your story is written in *scene*, not in *summary of scene*. No distinction can be more important.

⇒

I HOPE THIS sounds as easy as it is practical and that you will get the hang of it. However, for those of us who are used to having our paws on things, it will take work to get back to being basic. Scene before summary, we all explain, and yet we all feel we need to explain what a scene wants to be before we allow it to go ahead and demonstrate itself.

We *all* do this, especially when we are starting out to write a book. Our motive is simple: We're trying to sound confident.

We're usually really trying to sound like *authors*, which is harmless enough except when it drives the story back underground just as it is trying to get started. We think a story must know its own *Beginning* and that this Beginning is where we need to start writing, so we get busy trying to write something Beginning-ish, which we guess we might cast as a prologue.

This happens—and it is very common—because we're trying to set out from the wrong place in the narrative geography, trying to guess, then guess again, where to *begin* this story of ours. We aren't realizing that one of the more basic truths is that any true Beginning will very naturally be hard to find.

The Beginning is actually doing its best to remain mysterious and will stay out of sight, at least until you've written the scenes that lie far along in the storyline. Your still-hypothetical Beginning hides because it's actually a very important narrative destination.

It is only later, after you're well into the story that you begin to catch glimpses of the Beginning, where it actually resides, all the way down there, half hidden by its own *Ending*.

In the architecture of the novel, this is always so: An Ending and its Beginning are integrally related, which you already instinctively know from reading good books, seeing good plays, watching good movies. We physically *feel* a resolution as every narrative mystery is finally addressed; we *feel* the Ending's reverberation all the way back down the storyline to the Beginning, the two united and shining one light on every event and incident to illuminate all meaning.

But you must get to the end of the story to feel that sense of having arrived at this destination. A Beginning and its Ending are two ends of the clasp on a necklace—it is the tension formed by the separation of these two all-important elements that gives power to your story. We feel when the two come together, like the final door to the story slides shut.

Architects call this sensation *closure*.

But because this is structural, a connective skeleton, it belongs to plot. Any of the many plot concerns we meet in this section need to be put aside for now, until Chapter 3. Plot's relationship to story doesn't concern us until we've accumulated enough narrative material for the elements themselves to begin asking for the coherence of structure.

⇒

AND THE TASK at hand now is so much simpler and more direct, so much easier to conceptualize than worrying about the ways a novel's plot differs from its story and the infinite variations on all of plot's structural complexities. With story we simply need to worry about time and place, tense, tone, and point of view.

For now our job is small enough to remain completely manageable. It's so easy, in fact, that you should do it right now.

All you need to do is write a scene that lies somewhere in the *neighborhood* of what might turn out to be your storyline. Go do this one immediate and concrete task, spending as little time as you can thinking about it beforehand, and no time at trying to write well. Make sure the writing doesn't sound large or grand—and more like something that would be easy to throw away.

You write one scene, remembering that this takes place *in action only*, that this scene consists of incidents and events that take place only before the direct witness of our senses: those we can see, hear, touch, taste, smell.

It may help to think of this exercise as *pre*writing, making sure it's the kind of writing that no one else needs to see.

With this simple act you've started to write a novel.

And you will need to free yourself by adamantly ignoring every structural concern, particularly those technical and architectural aspects we've touched on above. Your only worry right now is the need to ground yourself in your story's concrete sense of its own physical proximity, to begin in its specificity of time and place. What you'll immediately find in your scene is a feeling of physical intimacy.

You get to this scene by going directly to that intersection of time and place in which your story comes alive. You write the scene from *within* this scene, as its events and incidents transpire before your *haptic, or bodily, senses,* the manner that works best to make us feel these events are actually happening with us as witness.

⇒

YOUR STORY, FOR now, exists only in its scenes: The more ancient word for scene is episode, and we are dealing here with narrative truths that are very, very old.

Episodes *always* and *only* exist at their own very specific narrative locations, which are both fixed and identifiable. An episode occurs for a reason, which is always this: Something is just about to happen.

Remember Gigi from Chapter 1? Maybe she has begun to exert this narrative pull on us, as if she is becoming the mystery we're going to have to get down into the episode to solve:

The girl stepped from the bright parking lot into the fragrant gloom of the bodega. A man in a singlet stood behind the counter, watching Spanish-language TV. The volume was low, but she could hear a few words she knew.

"Can I help you?" the man asked, in completely unaccented English. He asked this without really glancing at her. He seemed to be about thirty years old.

"You know someone named Gigi?" the girl asked. "Someone told me she might be here."

"Lots of girls named Gigi," the man said, turning to stare at her.

"No there aren't," she said, looking back at him just as directly. "Not where this one comes from."

We simply go into the room of time, and the story itself seems to exist as if it's *streaming*. We fall into that piece of narrative that is always found in an *exact time and place*. We fall into the presence of the narrative and write it from within the scene.

And whenever we get lost—this happens inevitably and often—we need only remember that our story needs to physically stand someplace, that it must be a definite somewhere instead of an anywhere, that a story breathes in and breathes out just as we do.

Whenever we feel lost or entangled in the vastness of narrative time that our novel may seem to want to explore, we simply reset our sights away from the long view, which is trying to speak of what all this *may become*, and get back to the present, to the place we belong.

This is always a specific place, which is where the story is already enacting itself. This place and time lies somewhere along the storyline but is always in the narrative Now.

We start out with a story's simplest elements: actions demonstrated by incidents and events. We witness these actions *in scene*, as we're taking this scene by scene, as scenes are all your story consists of. And we're writing it *in scene* because we've set out to write the story only. This forces us to remember the most elemental *storytelling* method we are using when writing this novel.

At first we'll remain entirely dependent on the enactment of those narrative moments that need to be particularized in their own living time. A scene is written for the same reason: that in it something happens and that whatever this something is will be meaningful.

That a story consists of only its meaningful dramatic episodes is one of the oldest and most basic of narrative truths.

We learn to write in episodes because this is easy to tackle and because a novel is lifeless without them. Writing *in scene* forces us to physically create the story's narrative time and place. At first it might seem easier to stand to the side of the scene—as if peering into its room of time through a window and turning to tell us what you see—because it is simply easier to talk *about* a story and its action than it is to *re-create* it.

We all do this, which we can forgive as our natural tendency to lapse into explanation. All we must do to remedy this is to stop looking through the window at the scene, to go to the door and turn the handle. The door will open, and when it does, we step into the architecture of the story's already hot, bright room.

⇒

AS WE BEGIN, the scenes that come to us may not seem to link to one another in any kind of logical way. This shouldn't trouble us, as a story has its own way of following its own sequencing and narrative *cause and effect*.

In fact, your story already knows all about narrative cause and effect and has a highly developed sense of its own chronology, so we try to cede control of these matters to the story itself.

The story often seems to proceed by its own very private narrative strategy, maybe working in a linear manner to go along with an orderly chronology. Or its organization may feel spatial, as if it's putting itself together by patchwork. It may conform to its own secret floor plan, spiraling outward from a central narrative event.

These are the first intimations of the story's close personal relationship with plot, which will eventually fit like hand and glove. What we do right now is simply note this relationship without becoming overly distracted or preoccupied.

All we're doing right now is to work as quickly and uncritically as we can to arrive at a *provisional draft.*

A provisional draft is simply that: It's made up of writing you'd be happy enough to throw away. It should contain scenes and notes on scenes written in the kind of active language that allows the story to begin to enact its dramatic events. These actions take place so writer and reader both sense that we've entered the scene's room in time and felt the heat on our bare skin.

Remember, this is the most simple task, and the writing here will want to not become ornate. A scene goes on for only as long as it has something new to say. A scene may be very short, taking only a paragraph to show what it needs to show. Some of your most effective scenes may be only a few lines long:

> The king dies.
> The queen dies.

⇒

As YOU WRITE *in scene*, you'll notice that your story will begin vying for control with you. You encourage this, because only the story itself can tell you what its scenes contain.

You write hastily, maybe feeling as if you're the first on the scene of an accident or are the only one still sober at the end of a party. You report on events as they play out in front of you. You want only enough detail to get you back to the scene when you return to it. If the action is taking place right in front of you, you won't have time to be writing carefully.

We have no real need of careful writing at this early juncture. For this reason I suggest you read my note in the entry on Anne Lamott's concept of the *Shitty First Draft*, or SFD—which, almost twenty years ago, in her monumentally helpful *Bird by Bird*, liberated me from the need to write beautifully. We have no use for all this good and careful writing right now, as beautiful writing weighs us down, becoming its own kind of burden. The real danger? We become *attached* to it.

The point of a provisional draft is simply to get the story sketched out *in scene*. This is why it contains the elements of story only. This is why this draft is called provisional.

We write this provisional draft to get as close to the bare-bones story as scene and scene alone, and this teaches us how to write *in scene*. It also helps break the worst authorial habit we all have: falling back into explanation.

Writing *in scene* allows you to explain nothing, which in turn frees you from having to worry about everything that your reader either does or doesn't know. This in turns frees you from all kinds of structural apparatuses that work along with the need to just explain a few things, including chapters, chapter titles, flashbacks, the importation of huge great chunks of background, flash-forwards, all our narrative bridges or pauses. We are freed from everything, then, that pulls the narrative up out of the moment at hand and all of which we come to later.

To start writing a novel is *exactly* this simple: You allow the scenes from your story, the story that has been bumping you and nudging against you as if it's emerging out of darkness, to itself begin to control the writing process. As it begins it wrests the reins of the narrative from you, and you begin to sense your story's absolutely amazing power.

When this happens your scenes will begin to seem to want to write themselves:

The girl stepped from the bright parking lot into the fragrant gloom of the bodega. A man in a singlet stood behind the counter, watching Spanish-language TV. The volume was low, but she could hear a few words she knew.

"Can I help you?" the man asked, in completely unaccented English. He asked this without really glancing at her. He seemed to be about thirty years old.

"You know someone named Gigi?" the girl asked. "Someone told me she might be here."

"Lots of girls named Gigi," the man said, turning to stare at her.

"No there aren't," she said, looking back at him just as directly. "Not where this one comes from."

"And where might that be?" he asked, his tone challenging.

"I know her," the girl said. "I know Gigi and I'm here to help her."

The man kept looking at her levelly.

"Lookit," the girl said. "I don't know if she's told you this but somebody's after her."

He said nothing.

"Someone aside from me, I mean."

The story takes off and begins to exhibit the same narrative energy that will power you through a provisional draft. We all share this power with every other storyteller, from ancient times through the present moment and on to those as yet unborn. We share it, too, with those who listen to our stories, and all of us understand this to be something ageless and completely inexhaustible.

In order to write your story's scenes, you need only trust it to behave as every story will. To trust this story, you need only begin to trust yourself.

⮑

YOU WRITE A scene, any scene. You do this by not worrying at all about finding your narrative river's hypothetical headwaters, but by wading from the safety of the shallows out into its stronger currents. You become reckless, you wade in anywhere, daring yourself to let go. You get quiet, trying to hear what there is to hear, to see what there is to see. Focus always on the side of the more mute part of yourself, which is the realm of your bodily senses. You try to turn your thinking off.

You seek refuge in the particular, beginning *in scene* and ending *in scene*. Whenever you feel lost, you immediately revert to scene, in order to rush through your SFD as quickly as you can, and the hurry with which you work may start to feel like time itself rushing along.

What defines this story as *your* story will be its direct attachment to its own very specific time and place, its foundation, its frame and footprint, so you write only carefully enough to honor a scene's specificity. The story's interest in this time and place will feel energized and heightened, reminding you that your story has shown up here for a reason. The story has a reason. Its reason is always the same:

Something is just about to happen.

So a story's mood is never reflective; it is always anticipatory, facing resolutely in the direction of its future. It is motivated by forces we don't actually understand but may have to do with curiosity and its inborn narrative momentum.

A story asks: *Why this day?*

Why this day? The answer will always be the same: Something's happening, something's revealed, then *something else* is going to happen.

⤳

IN ORDER TO trick your story into showing itself to you, you need only show up where it is already enacting itself, then place yourself in scene. You choose any scene anywhere along the storyline. You enter anywhere the ground floor or basement door seems willing to swing open.

You enter, and as you do your writing self will be trying to write a good-enough sentence that works to dramatize this scene by showing *exactly* what's going on in this specific time and place. You write this scene any way you need to in order to enter in a haptic, or bodily, way.

You need not expect that you know beforehand what these scenes contain. Their actions are the narrative reason for these scenes and may, only now—as you write them—start being revealed to you.

You write a sentence, then you write another one. To repeat: These don't have to be good sentences, and it may be better if they aren't. Good sentences—good writing of all kinds—slows a story down by making us self-conscious. Good writing often sounds as if it is trying to sound like literature, which is all well and good except that your story doesn't *care* about literature.

Our basic strategy is to work imagistically and in an auditory way, listening, asking our own bodily senses to center us, to locate us within the scene. It is by working with sensory materials that we encourage the writing on the page to help itself forget that it is a construct of language.

As you relinquish yourself to scene it will seem to come alive before your eyes in a manner rivaled in our waking moments only by IMAX 3D. You enter it spatially, as you would a waking dream.

Which is *exactly* what happens when we do actually dream. Our rational selves are forgotten, and we're carried along by sensation alone, rushed by the same narrative current that works always to solve itself. Dreams move as our stories do, in the direction of their inevitability, which is where they can, at last, unravel their own confusion.

This current, however, may feel dangerous, as if it's something our waking selves can neither control nor contain. This narrative current gives us the feeling that these stories of ours do not, in fact, exactly belong to us, as they lie slightly outside the grasp of reason.

It feels like I'm being carried along by it, a student told me recently, *like I've completely lost my foothold.*

Exactly, I said. *This means the story itself has taken charge.*

The energy of our scenes seems to preexist, as if it supersedes us and almost wants to evaporate the selves we've been working all our lives to carefully construct.

No wonder we are afraid of it.

⇒

ALLOWING THE STORY its own sense of direction is, however, exactly what we need to have happen. We keep the blueprints in the tube. This shows that we have stopped listening to ourselves in the act of writing and have started the sleepwalk trudge up the stairs toward the brink of that deep well where we fall off into sound and image and bodily sensation. Story places us exactly down in that tumbler of scene requiring only our witness.

So we try to sit down as bravely as we can, to enter our story's scenes by any means we can manage. We rely on our own bodily sensations to bridge the two realities, to get there in a way that we begin to feel the three-dimensionality of the scene. We give the job of witness to an entity we'll call *the noticer*.

The noticer has nothing more than the most rudimentary point of view, all your story initially requires. We're not worrying about the architecture and complication of perspective at this juncture, as this is all provisional. Point of view becomes almost instantly complex as well as technical, lying outside the small and immediate rooms of story.

For now all we need is a noticer who's located down within the scene, acting as our eyes and ears—someone positioned exactly where they must stand to give us this episode's news.

The noticer, right now, needs to be either that most uncomplicated form of first person (the one with no name, no agenda, no interesting backstory) or the kind of intimate third person that feels as intimate as the first.

You ask this noticer to act like a sensate 3-D camera, able to see the scene but also witness hot, cold, wet, dry, as well as every meaningful action:

"Lookit," the girl said. "I don't know if she's told you but somebody's after her."

He stared.

"Someone aside from me, I mean . . . "

The man picked up the lid on a plastic cake plate filled with baked meringues.

"Want one?" he asked.

"No thanks," she said.

He bit into the baked white fluff, roughly the size of a baby's fist. Tiny flakes fell around him like snow's minor afterthought.

The actions in this scene seem meaningful. The drama of the moment seems to require them, in that the man behind the counter must *do* something to mark the time it takes him to figure out if the girl who has come into the bodega asking for Gigi can be trusted.

He does something, eating, that makes him seem harmless; he also offers the girl something, as if he's a host, which lets her know he is no longer understanding her to be a threat. Because she understands that she's been accepted, her vigilance relaxes. This we sense, instead of being told: She's allowed a moment in which to have a thought. It is by the action of her thoughts—the girl is the *noticer* in this scene—that we understand how big the meringue is and what its texture is like. Her relief allows her a moment to think metaphorically.

How can an action be meaningful? By having consequences on down the storyline. The consequences of this incident or that event will either be obvious to us or hidden behind the domino race of cause and effect. We simply trust the story to remember that we will need to come to the all-important matter of consequence *eventually*. Here we're trusting this man, suddenly, to become a friend or helper or confidant. It is by virtue of his actions that we understand him to be trustworthy.

But we try not to overthink all this. We don't want to be too involved in either cause or effect or an action's consequence right now, as the story's narrative future is just a plot concern. Story cares only about the Now, defined by the chunk of narrative time we find in the scene at hand.

We also do not worry, while in a scene, about what's *led up* to this scene. Background doesn't concern us, because background—if it's meaningful—will always find a way to pop up in your story's present time.

You set your noticer loose to *witness* the scene, which you write *in scene* instead of *summary of scene*. Summary is another plot device, which we'll later use to speed us along through those flat places where nothing meaningful is occurring.

Getting into the scene in the deep and intimate way I'm asking may feel like you're entering a place to which you haven't been invited—and aren't even certain you're allowed. To sneak into a story that doesn't exactly belong to you (because, as we've seen, your story belongs, more accurately, to itself) will indeed feel risky—you really don't know what you're going to discover in any particular room in time.

But you do need to feel exactly this close to your story's happenings to convincingly share these incidents and events with your reader. You yourself will need to *participate* in your scene's active time to involve your readers, who will enter the scene via *your* haptic, or bodily, experience of it. The feeling will be one of having your feet planted on this specific ground, your lungs filling with the air of *this* particular locale.

There is honestly nothing more important to your story at this early stage than its ability to pull its writer into a scene that makes this writer seem a willing *participant* in it. You will simply need to live your story's physical reality in exactly this visceral way for its scenes to do the work they need to do. They need to get us all to believe in them. The first person your story must convince is you.

A story's only purpose, aside from the act of telling itself, is to participate in its own sense of reality. The technical term for this is *verisimilitude*.

➡

YOU GET INTO the habit of going to where you find these scenes, moving in this narrative direction with discipline and regularity. You try to write day in, day out, which works to keep the sights and sounds of a story's scenes alive in the mind even when you're able to pay them little direct attention. If you can learn to fall asleep while visualizing the actions of your scenes, you'll find your storytelling mind will keep subliminally working as you dream.

And your story in its most raw form does feel like you are dreaming it into being. What's happening is that your story's episodes are laying claim to whatever narrative territories they need as they create their own geographical dimension, a very vivid sense of time and place. The dreaming mind does not actively differentiate between fact and fiction—it believes in itself in exactly the way a story will, feeling no palpable difference between what it sees and hears from what occurs in the cold, hard reality of the day-to-day.

So you try to get to this sleep/wake place as expediently as you can; you also try to write simply, elementally, of what you find there, letting your story show you what it holds, episode by episode, scene by scene. And you discipline yourself to stay free of the twists of narrative time that inevitably come along to entangle us. These time tricks need to occur later, after we're more certainly planted in what we'll increasingly feel to be our story's physical architecture.

For now, we do everything we can to resist tucking memories down into scenes, as this is almost always a not-very-tricky way of importing backstory. Backstory—like so much else the story very quickly brings to mind—is a *plot* concern.

This is also why we must free ourselves from any need to work in *chapters*. Chapters present their own kinds of structural problem, in that they tend to number themselves, when the scenes and episodes do not actually know the order in which they will eventually fall. Chapters are actually another time-management tool we're not yet ready for. Sometimes chapters can cement episodes into a kind of narrative time that will feel like an aggregate.

When starting out, you simply do yourself a huge favor by avoiding every organizational schema imposed from outside the story's moments—and yes, I do mean *all* overlays—even including, for now, outlines.

Working in episodes allows your story the haste and simplicity it needs to evolve into its own sense of time and place. You want to allow your scenes to present their own incidents and events to you as directly as possible.

Your scenes *want* to dramatize themselves. They'll *want* to contain at least two characters who are doing something aside from thinking. What these characters are doing is immaterial—it might be robbing a bank, talking to each other, or crossing a room to answer the door. These actions will need to feel like *physical* actions, something that can be placed before the witness of our senses. An action can be speaking *out loud*, saying words that can actually be heard and understood as dialogue.

You write a scene through to its conclusion, staying within the scene for as long as it takes to arrive at its own point. You write directly, treating narrative time in the most uncomplicated way by working, for now, in either the *simple past* or the *simple present*.

You remember to offer no opinions, no asides, no digressions or tangents, and allow no character to think long thoughts, since thinking great long thoughts almost always goes against a story's need to get to its next piece of action, and is usually a way of trying to import *background*.

Background, if ignored, will almost always take care of itself.

Your characters' thinking actually also tends to belong to plot, which will offer them pauses, rest stops, vestibules, and bedrooms later on along their journey, when our characters might have something to think about that's more useful to the story.

You'll make sure to set the characters down within your scene so that they understand themselves to be subject to its laws and rules. This means they operate according to the demands of the story's own map of narrative time and space. If they must remember something, they'll need to remember it *realistically*, not by lapsing into memory.

Memories are even trickier to write than thoughts, as they want to intrude and grow large and become their own little scenes and episodes (see *embedded memory*). These almost always belong to plot, and they place unnecessary weight in the truck bed of the narrative Now, which isn't useful if we're trying to encourage the story's onrush.

When a memory presents itself as a strong and vivid scene, simply write it as a scene and worry about where it goes on the line of the story later.

You stay *in scene* because the scene always contains something your story needs to say. Your attention to these moments alerts us to the dramatic nature of the narrative situation: Something's happening, and this *matters* to the story. Whatever is happening in this story, down in the building of Now, is happening because everything is just about to *change*.

⇒

So you write a scene, then write another scene, and quickly realize that they have begun to pace themselves. The actions you're discovering in your scenes are usually those normal activities of daily living that each of us already knows all about: we eat, drink, talk, brush our teeth, begin to raise our voices to yell down the hall, the landline rings. Your character will pointedly ignore the phone or physically walk across the room to answer it. Your noticer needs to see what happens.

A story is unlike our own ordinary existences, however, in one very important way: In every scene that you dramatize, the trajectory of the storyline will be slightly changed.

If the process of writing a provisional draft feels chaotic, this is because we're trying to let it loose and allow the part of us that explains everything to ourselves to be quiet for a moment. We're trying to stand on the side of mystery and be able to tolerate these mysteries, as we turn the story over to the story itself to tell. And yet—this is the beauty we will discover only through this process—nothing will ever be as random at it might at first appear.

Your story is, in fact, relentless in its wish to move logically, in its own clear direction, in order to meet its next moment of crisis, conflict, or change.

Whatever is happening is occurring *in order* to change what happens next, which is what makes a scene's actions meaningful:

There will be consequences that we cannot, at this moment, fore-tell. These consequences, however, will directly determine the narrative's future.

You will write this episode through the conflict it presents and on toward its next moment of conflict or crisis or change. You allow each scene to come to its own conclusion. You can write as roughly, as broadly, as cartoonishly as you need to. You need to speed through your provisional draft as quickly as possible.

Try not to reread your writing, as this has a way of asking you to rewrite, which will only slow you down. Try to worry as little as you can about *narrative logic*, as what might seem like a mistake in cause and effect is usually your story trying to teach you something that your scene wants you to realize.

Our stories are like our dreams in another way: They are infi-nitely smarter than you and I are about what they want to say.

You write your episodes, worrying not at all about whether they lie next to one another along the *narrative arc*. You come to these scenes as they present themselves for your noticer to wit-ness. You allow yourself whichever point of view—first person or third—feels most natural.

We begin in simple first or close third because these offer us the most direct access when we're trying for close proximity to a scene's action. An *omniscient point of view* belongs to plot, in that it allows for a narrator to assume a grand perspective to see all up and down the storyline. Omniscience is what we may come to after we *have* a storyline.

What you will almost immediately realize is that your story is not *only* telling itself to you; it has another aim in mind.

It is also teaching you how to write.

⇒

YOUR SCENE OFTEN advances itself upon you by its use of a single image. You'll see (as I am now beginning to) the baked meringues sitting on the counter of the bodega. The scene in the bodega springs from a memory I didn't know I actually even remembered. This was the little market on the corner of 14th and Webster, NW, down the street from where I lived in Washington, D.C. The family that ran this bodega were friendly but reserved, which—as I got to know them a little better—I believed stemmed from their being central to the Salvadoran community in the District of Columbia, where the concentric circles of interrelatedness helped to shelter illegals. They simply seemed to me like the people who would be caretakers.

So you do exactly this: You grasp an image or a sound out of the physical space of your cache—whatever has interested you enough to stash it in your book bag—and you offer it to the narrative. You use the trick of recalling a physical object (such as the meringues, which were homemade and sold for a quarter) to get your mind engaged by the mind-body opportunity that is the three-dimensionality of your story's reality.

And you do want to feel yourself surrounded by the physical sense of place in that one specific moment as you write your way forward into the scene. You pay extremely close attention to your sensory experience of this scene, your feet planted there and the air of the place smelling like . . . what, exactly?

You write the scene without worrying at all about what has come before. Story is not encumbered by the past and doesn't need to explain itself, because it exists only in its own simple present, that same Now that we turn over to the noticer to access.

As we write our scenes via their sounds and sights and physical objects, we suddenly feel that we have entered into the excitement of the narrative present, which feels dreamlike and vivid. Brain science can now tell us more than we've ever known about this process: Magnetic imaging shows that our stories lodge in *exactly* the same places as do dreamed images, the visual cortex lighting up with identical activity.

So we try to fall into our stories as regularly as we do our dreams and to be able to get there quickly by the twin mechanisms of comfort and belief. This is the same logic that has us almost entirely believing that brain science will—in the not-too-distant future—allow the real Jake Sully, in *Avatar*, to leave his physical body lying on life support in the module while his mind goes off to inhabit a much more beautiful and morally persuasive realm. The technical name for the work of the storytelling mind is *profluence*.

You seek always to create an intimacy, to get deeper *in scene*, to go further, to sense risk, to feel an ever-stronger sense of narrative immediacy, so you burrow directly into narrative time to see for yourself what your story holds. There will always be a reason your story has asked you here, as the scene contains something it needs for you to find.

You go there to discover yourself in the presence of your characters' reality, and they will operate—as in a dream—independently of you. You are learning to trust the logic of your story itself.

You stay *in scene* by concentrating on the who, what, when, and where—and on writing the episode's particulars as physically as you can. You write a scene only until it begins to show what it holds for you, allowing it to go from room to room following the *arrows of time*, which lead to the narrative's future.

Here we see what comes of an episode that's left to write itself. Here we have the germ of a story that has to do with hiding someone who has no wish to be found. From exactly this kind of particle of story, what is at least a subplot of a book can easily grow:

The girl stepped from the bright parking lot into the fragrant gloom of the bodega. A man in a singlet stood behind the counter, watching Spanish-language TV. The volume was low, but she could hear a few words she knew.

"Can I help you?" the man asked, in completely unaccented English. He asked this without really glancing at her. He seemed to be about thirty years old.

"You know someone named Gigi?" the girl asked. "Someone told me she might be here."

"Lots of girls named Gigi," the man said, turning to stare at her.

"No there aren't," she said, looking back at him just as directly. "Not where this one comes from."

"And where might that be?" he asked. His tone was challenging.

"I know her," the girl said. "I know Gigi and I'm here to help her."

The man kept looking at her levelly.

"Lookit," the girl said. "I don't know if she's told you but somebody's after her."

He said nothing.

"Someone aside from me, I mean."

The man picked up the lid on a plastic cake plate filled with baked meringues.

"Want one?" he asked.

"No thanks," she said.

He bit into the baked white fluff, roughly the size of a baby's fist. Tiny flakes fell around him like snow's minor afterthought. Just as he turned back toward the TV screen, he lifted his chin, then moved his head sideways to indicate. This was almost imperceptible, as if he was doing it against his better judgment, showing her how to go back.

"Go past the bathroom," he said, "and on up those stairs."

And suddenly here we are, embarked on a story that wants to lead up deeper into itself, wants us to climb the ascending stairs that lead always upward in search of *complication*.

Meaningful action can absolutely be depended upon to move in *exactly this way*, upward into what we'll find in the House of Plot, the architecture that our story itself will almost immediately begin to generate.

3

Plot

B Y LETTING THE story come first, we're simply trying to get its scenes to begin to show themselves to us. Our most basic motive is to allow these novels of ours to start to dream themselves into being, by letting them arrive in their own *affective state*, their own living, feeling natures.

But story, without narrative shape, so easily becomes nothing more than the tedium of *long story long*. A novel is distinguished not only by its large narrative size but also by meaning. We'll get to the novel's progression toward meaning—this is delivered by those demarcations we call Beginning, Middle, and End—later in this chapter. For now, let's examine the kind of journey we've set out upon, without dwelling on its length or how far we still have to go.

For now, nothing's different: We're still writing according to the same modus operandi, still allowing ourselves to sketch *any* episode that occurs to us, *any*thing that seems to lie *any*where along the line of the story. These scenes may begin to tell us something about their placement, but placement still isn't a worry. Right now we're still just entering into each episode as if it were one of the novel's many rooms of time.

And we'll want to start our next step—we call it *sequencing*—in this same relaxed and laid-back manner, simply showing up to those narrative spaces that our stories already seem to occupy. We're still writing to find the pulse of the story's Here and Now. We show up, get quiet, listen for directions. All we're doing is giving the story a chance to show us something more about itself. It will accumulate in the way of knowledge, and as it does, the story will begin to become directive, telling us where we need to go.

When I, for instance, take time to listen to what my story has to say—this is the one about the girl in the bodega with the little white dog in it hidden (I hope) somewhere down the arc of the narrative—my story says: *You head straight back there through the storeroom, see? Turn left, then take the second left past the restroom. That's where you find the stairs.*

The stairs? I think. Nope, I just really don't *think* so. I'm reacting automatically against anything that sounds hard. I have no real wish to be climbing anything that even *sounds* like *stairs*, thanks, especially those found in the shadows at the back of some strange building whose narrative purpose remains unclear to me, among characters I don't yet recognize and where I do not speak the language.

Nope, I say, in that climbing requires the concerted physical effort that I'm not sure I wish to expend. Nope, I want a guaranteed result. I'd rather stay out right here in the light of day, where it's safe, where it feels more ordinary, where my feet feel planted on the firmament that is story's still-horizontal-feeling ground. That would be the cement floor of the bodega, thanks, which—while imaginary—at least *feels* like a real time and place.

All this stalling comes from fear: None of us just naturally *wants* to go where we've never been before, and a novel is *necessarily* new and foreign territory. Even if you've written a book, even if you've written four or five books, as I have, your novel is here to tell you've never written IT before. Each book is the one that seems organized to defeat you, to remind you that you know nothing yet about its size, shape, length, or what it hopes to contain.

Each novel is, in fact, its own narrative republic, a different country, made up of all these different temporal and linguistic regions.

All your story is asking of you, right now, is that you keep an open mind. *Come on*, it says, *let's go see what there is to discover.*

The name of this impulse is *quest*—every good novel has one. Your little grouping of episodes has begun to intimate their own small truths about this quest. We *feel* this in our scenes, that they seem to be suddenly impelling us to move in a certain direction, following their fictional imperative.

The quest in the bit of story I've been writing takes the name Gigi. So far, we really have no idea who or what this Gigi person is or why we should be interested in her, only that her story lies somewhere off in *this* direction. We know nothing about her, not even her real name, we have no idea why she's making it hard to find her. In fact, we know only this: She is hidden. Her being hidden is the only salient detail we have.

Because of this property—we might call it her "enigmatic nature"—we know that Gigi belongs to plot.

Plot is the map of what's to be found in the territories that remain unknown. Plot is what gives a long story its novelistic feeling; it is the landscape that defines the country of the novel. We are evidently embarked on this kind of lengthy journey, one that has consequence, magnitude. We are off to the Brave New World, though we have *no idea* of what kinds of creatures—beauteous or otherwise—we're going to find there. We're going, though we're not feeling particularly brave at all.

Quest is the name of that larger, more *novelistic* sense a novel almost immediately starts to have, whereby scenes gather and clump and begin to speak among themselves like the travelers in Chaucer. All of a sudden scenes open out into other possibilities, as if they understand themselves to belong to something that's thematically larger than what they set out to be. A novel has scope, a grandeur, a seriousness of purpose.

And this—as you begin to climb the scary staircase at the back of the building—is why you may start hearing the carnival voices, doing their lost-in-the-funhouse laugh. *You don't know where you are, do you?* these voices ask. *You can't write a novel. You? You don't know what you're doing!*

That's right, you say, I haven't the *slightest* idea. This is the truest, deepest, most honest answer. All you know is that someone or something seems to be calling out to you, asking that it be found. So we allow ourselves to be led back into the shadows and up the rickety staircase, looking for a flashlight in a dark building.

Our writing still has a strange, cartoonish sense to it: ham-fisted, hilariously amateurish, our characters tend to seem so *exaggerated*—HAPPY! or SAD!—more like clowns than like people. We're still pounding on the keyboard, writing seven sentences to discard six. Nothing much is probably going right, yet we go on, drawn upward, moving *toward* what is confusing rather than *away* from it, working in a manner that lacks shape, clarity, subtlety. This is plot at work, but you can't know this yet because plot's part—in a Shitty First Draft—is to convince you that you don't know the first thing about *anything*.

And as you climb the stairs in back you need only remember the solitary nature of this enterprise, that you're going to have to allow yourself to dwell in your own book's narrative confusion.

Which is why the voices start in now—and why they didn't before. Before, we were just writing our modest scenes that didn't ask themselves to amount to much of anything.

But now our episodes are beginning to get organized; now they stand together to begin to create narrative dimension, a sense of power and self-importance. They seem to have a sense of their own logistics and strategy, giving you the first intimations of their potential.

We're noticing something now about the size and shape of their ambition, which is *novelistic. Look at Miss Fancypants*, my own voices chime in right about now. *Look at her*, they say, *trying to act like an important "novelist."*

What has happened is that these scenes and episodes have begun to coalesce into groupings that speak to one another down the hallways of narrative time. They have *big concerns*; they mean to cover *a lot* of territory, and they want to do this convincingly.

It's right about here, when it all starts to feel loud and cari-catured and warped-mirror *strange*, that we realize we've entered into the House of Plot.

⊇

BODEGA? IN CALIFORNIA, where I live, a *bodega* actually means something that more approximates storeroom. Around here, in a Spanish-speaking neighborhood, the little store on the corner is more likely the *tienda*; the open-air market's a *mercado*. The bodega? It's a wine bar in Europe, while in the big cities of the East Coast, only the corner grocery, the bodega, would hold a character like Gigi.

Why do I mention this? Because it's so very easy to get side-tracked as you enter the House of Plot in all these writerly diver-sions, whereby you allow your story to be linguistically hijacked, so you can stop doing what you're doing (which is being con-fused) and go do a little research. It's all *so very interesting!* It's also stalling. We stall because we're afraid to commit to the upward trudge, to confront the vast amounts of darkness at the top of the stairs, to take this darkness in, to admit that it pertains to us, to admit the first thing about the monumentality of what we don't know, that we cannot find out by using conventional research methods.

You skip past the part where you get busy Googling the word *bodega*, you suck it up, you head on back through the storeroom, past all that huge amount of narrative mess that *may* inform your story *eventually*, but is no help right now. This is stuff that no one may ever even know about, much less *see*, the gate of the house where the real problems can occur.

You take a hard left just past the place where there are stacks and stacks of that real Coke that's bottled in glass in Mexico, still being made with real sugar that is still made from real sugarcane (and you don't get stuck and distracted here by your need to research what's called the Columbian Exchange or even that one part of that whole huge and very terrible history of sugarcane production in the New World, responsible for not only the wretchedly foul and falling-out teeth of people of the British Isles but the entire West Indian slave trade).

Nope, you stop yourself. You see the stairs that you need to start climbing, the light is dim, the way is hard, and you're getting that sinking feeling.

This is because even *thinking* about plot will feel existentially confusing, which is why you'd much rather go research the transatlantic slave trade, which is *completely* depressing—but not as depressing as *plot*.

Plot confounds us, makes the novelist feel stupid, because it's conceptual. This is its most basic concept: You and I, as novelists, don't know *the first thing* about our book's own very natural plot-mindedness. In fact, plot and story are already in league together; they're already double-teaming us, and their joint aim is to win.

They're going to need to defeat us, at first, for our book to be any good.

So we need only start to *think* about plot in order to feel lost. The thoughts themselves feel headachey, difficult, in that they concern these abstract concepts that we cannot quite get our minds around. Where, for instance, does our story's Beginning lie and where *the hell* does all this random-feeling stuff go? And how does all this end up? Am I saying that we're really going to have go ahead and *write* all this to get through with it? *What?!* We have *to write* a whole long book-length thing to find out how it ends?

Are you *kidding me*?

The novel-writing enterprise—when you get to plot—starts to sound like a structural impossibility, that it's an instruction manual you have to write in order to be able to read how to begin.

Welcome to the funhouse. *Plot?* Most of us have better things to do. Me? I'm needed elsewhere; the top of the refrigerator, for instance, is dying to be cleaned.

⋑

FIRST WE WRITE the long story long; we write it any which way we can. We sneak up on it; we stalk it. We haze and subvert it. We overwhelm it with language, we do it wrong, start over, we do it wrong again.

We write long, and only then do we get to begin to rearrange it. It is in this restructuring and rearranging—what plot is—that your story will finally be made your own.

And the name of everything that does not show in your story is its plot, in that plot is your story's *structure*, its *architecture*—we tend to use the terms interchangeably. When you're finished with your novel, you will not really any longer *witness* all the labor that's gone into accomplishing its now-hidden engineering.

Instead, the structure of your book will seem to float in the mind in the nearly invisible way a beautiful building does, in that the way its architectural solution is so much a part of what this building has become that the structure and its design become synonymous, and the architecture asks to be ignored.

The structure of a good book allows its plot to vanish into its story, the two so seamlessly joined that they're separately unimaginable.

So you operate on trust, you put your head down, take a left, another left, past the stacks of dusty *hecho en Mexico* Cokes. You climb the stairs, thinking all the while about how you'd so much rather be home writing your treatise on the West Indian slave trade or your latest fair-to-middling poem or that one short story of yours that *might* get published after it's been workshopped another hundred times. You want to be doing *anything* that might give you a sense of mastery: inventorying Coke bottles, cleaning fridge tops.

What no one says is how many novelists cannot write a good short story to save our lives, that we've failed, too, as poets. This is why we fail when we try to work in the shorter forms: Our minds don't work like this. We're simply *interested* in the whole grand scheme of things, in entire histories and migrations, in centuries and generations, how one item (sugarcane) and the typical British person's love of sweets had all these devastating ecological and sociological consequences. This is what we're like: We are interested in huge events, in epochs and entire populations, which is why we require whole great swaths of temporal and narrative geography, because we're *novelists*, and we were probably born this way.

Here's the good news: It is much easier for people like you and me to write a good novel than it will ever be for us write a really good three-minute song. And our form—its largeness—is designed to accommodate our inborn sense of life and love and history because our books can be as big as they need to be to hold all that already exists in our hearts and souls. So we go on up the stairs because we are *like this*, we are *interested* in the process of discovery.

And because we are writing LARGE, we learn to tolerate our own lostness and inexactitude, the funhouse-mirror look of our cartoonish characters, who are BLOND, who have BIG BLUE EYES. We tolerate our oh-so-obvious little protoplots in which everything's fake, the GOOD PEOPLE just so *good*, the EVILDOERS exuding the coal-dark reek of evil.

A novelist has to be allowed to bumble around on the store-room staircase, confused by the semidarkness. The novelist learns to be amused by his or her own mistakes, that big blue eyes is shorthand for *nice*, which is shorthand for we *like* them. Everyone has written something as careless as "big blue eyes" a time or two; we'll do it again. But so what? No novel has ever *died* from it. We're learning by trial and error; we're learning by trusting our stories, even when they're leading us where we don't really want to go, which is up these darkened, cobwebby Stephen King–ish stairwells at the back of this ratty-looking building.

Why are we here? Because the plot and the story have ordered us to be.

⇒

OK, SO WE'VE climbed the stairs at the back of the storeroom in order to enter the House of Plot and . . . ?

We usually find ourselves exactly *nowhere*. We cannot find ourselves, we can't see our hands in front of our faces, so we fall back to writing this writerly stuff that begins to intone *It was the best of times, it was the worst of times* to remind ourselves we're still The Author.

This narrative locale is so often someplace we can't begin to recognize, a shadowy hallway lined with identical doors leading off as far as we can see, lighted only by twenty-watt bulbs flickering like they fully intend to burn out on us.

Where is this, *exactly*? And why is this confusion being churned up right when we're beginning to think we were actually getting somewhere? We are confounded because we're allowing ourselves to entertain thoughts and feelings about the novel's *structure*, which is inherently confusing. We are, after all, asking ourselves to design a building that's meant to house something that does not yet exist—in a place and time that *also* cannot quite yet be imagined.

⇒

STORY GIVES US bodily sensations, those that locate us securely within the specifics of a scene's three-dimensionality. The scene imparts to us a sense of its own self-confidence, in that we know we are in this particular Here and Now; we know where we're getting the air we need to breathe.

But plot, as we've seen, is story's opposite; it is an intellectual pursuit that gets theoretical and vague almost immediately, the moment we start to talk about it. Story has a present-tense sense to it: He comes, she sees, it conquers. Plot drifts back and back, getting all tied up in its tripping over the past-ness of its layered tenses, which sometimes seem like sheets of mica, and also include a concept, a tense, so far outside our cognitive reach it's even called the future perfect.

Plot is story's setting, its foil. It is story's counterpart and its antagonist. We are currently confused because plot wants us to be confused. If story is concrete, then plot—always, always—is being confusing and vague on purpose. It imparts to us, by every one of its infinite and very subtle clues, the notion that the world is unpredictable, tipped, and tilted—that reality itself is nebulous, that we cannot know the future, that it's futile even to try.

It is in the nature of plot to feel complicated and beyond the reach of our understanding. If story *is either/or*, plot confuses by saying *both/and*. It's disquieting, off-kilter, which is why we'd rather get out the spritz, the paper towels, and go climb a kitchen step stool.

This is, however, a confusion we are going to need to get used to. You need to remember this, so you might want to write it in ballpoint on your hand:

Plot will hide what story works very naturally to reveal.

⇒

THAT I-CAN'T-CLAP-IN-RHYTHM-LET-ALONE-DANCE SENSE we get when we begin to write a novel comes from the inexpert tension that develops between the dancing pair—story and its plot, plot and its story. They are trying to dance but cannot—right now—settle on who is supposed to lead.

So for this next step in the process of getting a provisional draft down on paper, we'll be writing on our hands in ballpoint, roaming anywhere, showing up wild-eyed, hair all which way, clothes askew, letting our pupils adjust to the darkness. We learn to tolerate our own clumsiness, our tripping over our two left feet, to tolerate our own sense of profound stupidity: I started writing this book without even really knowing what a *bodega* is? This is embarrassing! We tolerate our ignorance, our bumbling confusion. Having entered the House of Plot, we realize that it is axiomatic that rabbits run by us in top hats with pocket watches, and we take these for our inventions, thinking for a sec that we've caught sight of the Chihuahua we've been looking for. We do not know where we are—we don't even know *who* we are—and this makes our heads hurt and reminds us that we need to take a nap.

We're operating on blind faith that we're going to get somewhere, *trusting* that this will all work out. We go down the hallway, doing what a novelist will always do, which is turn the doorknobs. This is who we are: We get interested in reading the painted-on labels on the little, eight-ounce Cokes; we notice things because we're novelists, we're writing novels because this is what helps us figure out what all this means, when all the small pieces begin to fit together.

We're trying the doorknobs, most of which are locked, but we will—if we keep at it—come upon the one that turns. We are working in what feels like a layered and filmy darkness made up of filaments of time bonded to other filaments of time. The process is staggeringly hard: It may take days, weeks, months, and, in my case, always *years*.

It will almost always feel like the hardest thing you have ever done.

But finally, a doorknob turns, your story swings open, and you step in. The scene shows itself in exactly that moment of specific time where you need to be, so you can understand one small thing that begins to say something: A door slams, you hear a snatch of music that can be only *her* music, and you suddenly get that you do already know how this whole thing works.

We need to become hopelessly lost in the House of Plot in order to find our way out. This is how we learn, alone in the dark and by the touch of our own blind fingertips, how our book is going to shape itself.

⇒

IT IS SO easy to understand story's part of the narrative because it is characterized by the singularity of its events. Time will never be exactly like this ever again. It is only in this one so very specific moment that this piece of episodic time exists. It is our knowing that it is transient that makes it shine so brightly, that even as we apprehend it, it is being simultaneously lost to us.

We've become used to the three-dimensionality of living time within these scenes, and we now can enter them, look around, feel ourselves to be alive within a narrative that is being perceived in *exactly* this spatial way.

Scene is essential—your book is dead without it. It is also, however, only one layer of what will finally become the overlying tissues of narrative that will be stacked, like mica, down inside your novel. There is so much else in a novel that has nothing to do with scene, so much that lies outside that bright room, in the storeroom, the stairwell, the dim light of the hallway where we can barely see the clue we've written on our hand in ballpoint:

Plot will hide what story works very naturally to reveal.

⋑

THE NAME OF everything hidden is plot. This is your book's structure, and remember that we're using the terms *plot* and *structure* interchangeably. We don't want, finally, to see the structure of our book at work; we want for its architecture to operate as silently as it is currently asking us to proceed: blindly, quietly, efficiently.

So let's look at concrete examples offered by the story that started off to tell itself about Gigi's quest, which might be her looking for the Chihuahua mix and our then going out to look for her. We're upstairs in the rooming house we've found by going up the back stairs in the bodega's storeroom. Still we have no real idea of who or what Gigi represents, only that we need to find her.

If story exists in the rooms along the hallway, those rooms in which we're going to *eventually* find what we've been looking for all along (and in a novel, this is almost always something you didn't realize you'd lost), then *plot is the order by which we come upon our story's rooms*. This means a novel's structure will consist of the manner in which you set out its story's narrative sequence.

Ordinal structure is the sequence marked by *first, second, third*. This is the sequence that tells us when and where an action falls along the plotline. Your book's storyline, meanwhile, determines what comes first in the novel's *cardinal structure*; you must learn to be quiet now and let your book tell it to *you*.

This means that you cannot actually start writing a book by writing Chapter 1, Scene 1, because you don't yet know what Chapter 1, Scene 1 will need to contain. Story governs the ordinal nature of the narrative, while plot is devoted to the cardinal. Plot assigns order so it doesn't have to tell us what it knows about causal events and their relationships.

It is the order of a novel's events that shows us what it finds meaningful.

Plot—we will keep repeating this—works to hide what story is dying to show, and plot tricks us with its ability to look like it is story, so it will place an event in such a casual manner that we fail to recognize the significance of these events. We write a draft of a book in order for plot to show us how much of *everything* we're missing the first time through. Plot hides in plain sight; plot shows off that things are not what they seem, that we cannot know what anything means until we've experienced it over the long haul.

The job of your novel's plot is to show us—by way of demonstration rather than by pointing and shouting—this echoic, repetitive, gathering sense by which we gradually move toward an understanding of significance. A novel can earn its length—its right to feel the breadth and depth and width that will contain all it needs to contain—only if its length is balanced by the weight of its own meaning. Otherwise: long story long.

Plot is the context into which we place our story's events. Story is vital, but without context its events cannot be *meaningfully* understood. Story tells us what happens, while plot tells us what we're *to make* of these events.

Structure provides the story with its shape and size; it grows as a story grows in order to accommodate all that narrative volume. Without structure to order a story's events into their *meaningful* sequence, we'll feel lost in the continual present, the relentlessness of the Now. The Now that never ends feels too much like real life—we read *novels* to escape from it.

Marking your story's particular events by saying they are important in the larger sense is the job of your novel's structure. Plot is what lifts a story's scenes from their own mundane existence, in which, day after day, this happens, then this happens. Tragedy, even violent death, even violent death on a massive scale, even genocide: They are all worn away by the day-after-day nature of time. Time passes. We witness this. The evidence surrounds us. Every mass grave is eventually scattered, the bones it holds pulverized, its history erased, and this is one more reason there are novelists.

Plot is the way the novel gets around time's wish to level everything, to yawn, to intone the latest trite homily: *It is what it is (shrug); shit happens; water under the bridge, man; sand through the hourglass.*

Plot is what counteracts time's need to drone on endlessly. Plot is what says, *Hey! Listen! This actually matters, so you're going to have to begin to pay attention!*

SO PLOT IS story's sequence—the 3, 2 ,1 or the 2, 3, 1 of its scenes. These are events arranged not necessarily in the order in which they chronologically happened. Rather, they are positioned so they best show us what we are to understand about each event in the moment in which it occurs. Sequencing has everything to do with the way plot weaves layers of time, working with its transparency. We can then look back, through time that has already passed, to later understand an event's significance—and only later, when we encounter meaning in the story's narrative future.

For now all we're doing is looking for Gigi; we are examining the order by which we arrive at the story's individual rooms of time. It is plot's job to organize what is seen in these rooms, not only the order in which we come to them but *what* is noticed by this scene's noticer.

Plot lets story show us what's there. It shows—and does not tell—why we're needing to visit this room *right now*. These visits draw meaning to them. In a novel, knowledge is allowed the time it needs to accumulate, in the experiential way that mimics how we learn in life.

Knowledge in a novel is a process that plot allows to build.

So we can learn to think of process as the wind that moves over the place of story and must always exist in spatial form. We follow the plot as we might follow weather over a novel's territorial map. *It's here*, plot says, *at X marks the spot where we turn left and begin to climb the stairs.* We do this because plot and story are conjoined and time and place have become synonymous.

Here, your novel says, as you make it to the third floor and go halfway down to the third room on the right; the door's unlocked, it swings wide. *OK?* plot says to story. *Step up now and show us what we're seeing out the window. Show us what happens in this room that is giving this long thing meaning.*

The noticer notices what will advance the feeling that we belong in this room, to discover here the next thing we need to know about this story. It is by the act of our noticer's noticing an object—say, the radio on the nightstand or someone's red potted geranium—that indicates that this object has significance in our story. Plot hears everything, sees everything; plot knows, for instance, which song is playing on the radio. Plot either does or doesn't allow story to sing these lyrics aloud, because these lyrics either will or will not offer clues to the scene's significance.

Plot is also everything that *isn't* shown in a scene or episode, the hours of radio that spill meaninglessly (because they are unheard) into the empty room, vacated when Gigi split—and she *has* split. It is also *all* of those actions that lie off the direct line of the narrative, events necessary to the story (Gigi split) in their unseen, unheard energy.

So the plot of *The Iliad* contains the ten years of the Trojan War that have already been fought and so *need not be shown now.* The plot organizes the story so that it begins in medias res, in the war's final moments. Why? Because we cannot tolerate a ten-year-long war played out in real time, day in, day out, becoming mundane as time wears it down to the meaninglessness that says bones pulverized equals the grains in the sand of time.

What is important is that time here is being brought alive because the war is *ending!* Plot cares about Endings and Beginnings in the same way we do: Each is vitally important. It is this war's ending that offers meaning backward, all down the ten long years of the war that have already taken place.

Plot offers your story its moral, historical, spiritual, symbolic situation. Plot is where we get its emphasis, its nuance, its subtlety. We'll need to have language to allow the story to whisper itself to us. *The Iliad* requires certain words and names and phrases: *Achilles. The Muses, Trojans, besieging Greeks, priest of Apollo, captive of Agamemnon.*

Plot is the book that writes this language.

⇒

PLOT IS DIFFICULT to talk about because the discussion becomes so easily abstract. Story's concrete, that hot bright room where we can find ourselves, walk around, water the fern that Gigi left when she took the geranium, turn the radio down. Story is where we find comfort, while plot tends to trip us up on the edge of the carpet our feet stumble over in that long dark hallway.

Plot knows, for instance, where Gigi is right now, hiding, but it will not tell us.

Plot is also mechanically connective in ways we'll explore in technical detail in our next chapter, "The Mechanics of Narrative Time." It is the novel's temporal engineering, those essential architectural elements: the building's plant, its plumbing, wiring, floor plan, fire-escape routes; its square footage; its occupying a quarter of a block in the District of Columbia, which was laid out by Benjamin Banneker, this country's first civil engineer, who was African American, a freed slave. That the building was built of brick and mortar in the housing boom that followed World War II, that its plans are registered in the National Building Museum, nobody needs to know.

Or maybe, because we're novelists who may be working in a scale so large, we may need to know all that we are incidentally learning: that in addition to the bodega, there are seven other storefronts, each occupied, two of which are currently inhabited by large and extended families living in questionable circumstances, paying the rent, when they pay it, off the books, sharing the one lavatory down the hall.

Plot is also the alleyway out back, where a truck cab, late model, nice, on lease from a drayage company, is idling, its door painted with J&K MOVING, standing in a way that blocks the entire drive, so we know that the driver won't be long. We know this because he has left the cab unlocked, keys in the ignition. The engine's running because it's a hot day at the end of May, and the truck needs the air conditioning.

Plot is what draws our attention upward as we listen for the distinctive yip of a Chihuahua. There seem to be people moving around up there—are they bodega people, Salvadorans, harboring illegals? Plot is the history of the civil war in El Salvador. It's also what you and I have stuffed on the top shelves of closets of our own rooms, where we stash our own insecurities and secrets, our own ignorance—because we're Americans and largely buffered from the state of the world. There is this shameful fact: I cannot remember enough about the civil war in El Salvador of the early '80s to understand what I'm to do with the family who owns the bodega where Gigi has taken refuge. Are they kind to her because they, too, were refugees? Plot is what we'll use to get around what we don't know, what we'll still get to discover. Plot is what puts the walls around what's known in one room of time in the most efficient way. Plot lets us write moments of transit from room to room in summary of scene. It lets us skip the entire Trojan War, the whole long history of the CIA's involvement in Central America, and everything else we need to skip (for now) because it still lies off the line of the story.

⊃

SUMMARY OF SCENE was invented so the audience of Greek drama wouldn't have to sit through a blow-by-blow reenactment of all ten years of war. Plot uses summary of scene because our story has a past that it doesn't need to revisit in mind-numbing detail, because a story isn't interested in walking down the same second-floor hallway over and over, knocking on doors trying to find Gigi when she was staying on the third floor anyway and has already left, which you can tell when you see that her geranium's gone.

Summary of scene allows us to skip all those huge chunks of time where nothing interesting happens, my great-uncle, who was CIA, who drank too much, going on and on, blah-blah-blah about the U.S. presence in El Salvador.

Summary of scene is an absolutely *vital* element of plot because it lets us drift off, to go read in the bathroom while Uncle Bobby talks, to lock the door and look up stuff on Wikipedia that isn't as boring as listening to all that same crap. Plot lets us escape out the window of the bathroom when they come to look for us, to zone out on tall white men, their blah-blah loudness, to avoid visiting all those echoing empty rooms, to zoom—by narrative dream—past every dead part of our story's journey.

➤

PLOT EXISTS IN the novel because of the story's need for sequence and ranking and logic. *Ranking*—placing an episode first in a sequence of scenes—says, Lookit, this is really important. We don't have to say it's important; we know it is—because we've placed it where it is prominently displayed. Plot—eventually, but not exactly now—will say, This particular room is the most important room of all, because this is where the story metaphysically starts. The story, then, begins right here, X marks the spot. In the circular metaphysics that a novel's narrative organization will ultimately reveal to us, we come to the end of our novel only when we find out how it starts.

Beginnings? Endings? The mechanics of narrative time? These always get us into trouble, which is why we don't even start trying to talk about them until we've been working at this awhile. It's as if a Beginning and an Ending have always lived together in domestic partnership in the same room of time, a room that plot and story have come over to visit again and again. The trouble is, in starting out, we can never tell which room this is.

Which means only that we're going to have to keep on writing our episodes in any order that they occur to us for another little while, knowing that when we come to this most important room of all, the radio will be loud and that the room will be decked out to shine in its significance. Room 307 will be all lit up in neon that reads *GIGI! GIGI! GIGI!*

So we're in the House of Plot, still writing scenes in whatever order. This almost inevitably will *not* be the order in which these events have happened, because the narrative wants to work across time and space as if it's a map of a land that lays its claims spatially. The narrative works sideways, going by the dream logic of storytelling, which is associative. It says this sits *next to this* in time, rather than *behind* or in *front* of each other. Our stories are actually unruly; when you try to put them in chronological order, they act like kindergarteners who won't line up.

If your story seems to want to skip around and back and forth and around and through its own chronology, it's because it knows how fun this whole thing can be. It's recess; the story has the map of the place so well in mind that it's a game of tag, a time for hide and seek. Rigidly lining up is predictable, and a story cannot be predictable, or everyone quits and goes home.

We might set out to tell the story in chronological order, *this* happens, then *this* happens. But plot and story have already left the premises; they've grabbed their geranium and gone out the third-floor window. They're already imagining themselves a hundred miles away west, in a moving truck on Route 80 on its way to Nebraska, carrying thirteen tons of household furnishings.

So plot and story will begin—if given the chance—to work together to tell us the order in which we're to enter those bright rooms where we find our scenes. Plot likes to take apart chronological order and mess with it, to redraft the footprint of the building at 14th and Webster we thought we'd already built back in the days after the Second World War.

But now it's suddenly saying we have to move the stairs from *inside* the building to outside, that this involves escape routes, building codes. Now we must have these switchback flights running in a series of half stories, with landings all the way to the roof. That's because we need a place for the Salvadoran refugees to hang out their wash, also a spot where they can lay these seemingly random objects: the clay flowerpots holding the bright red geraniums, the hibachi, the rag mop set upside down to dry.

Plot says we will eventually enter the rooms upstairs in the order that tells us their meaning, but we cannot know that order yet because we haven't arrived in the rooms that show us—by the clue of the potted geraniums—exactly where the story's headed.

Story works associatively, by placing two objects—the radio tuned to Gigi's station and the red geranium—next to each other in the manner of a painting: These things go together in some wordless manner that plot and story will leave to us to figure out.

Plot works associatively too, putting two chunks of time next to each other in this same painterly way. Two episodes, side by side, will soundlessly reverberate. We *know* these elements are related because they stand next to each other in the halls of time. It is important that they do so. It's important because the noticer has noticed that they do.

⇒

JUST AS STORY and its wisdom accumulates, plot works with time to render its meaning progressively. We will, along the line of this story, encounter another red geranium, which will rhyme in our minds with the one on the back steps of the boarding house we found by going out into the alley behind the bodega, where the moving truck's cab is still idling. There's that hot diesel smell. The trucker, whose name is Bob McGaw, who drives out of Baltimore, has the air conditioning going. In Ball-a-mer they call it the AC.

Plot says you're wandering in an alleyway of this eastern city just south of Baltimore, in which you know no one. Plot says you're seventeen years old, a girl. Plot says you were born here in the United States, but you still do not really *feel* like you speak the language. Plot says that this isn't just another of your little stories, that it has started to feel like a great adventure, that this is a *novel*, that it wants to make a big, American-feeling-story kind of sense of itself.

Every novelist I have ever known has this large *American-feeling* sense about the size of his or her stories. Plot says we're novelists, which means that we all feel like this, like we're both *huge* and simultaneously *no one*.

But now you're becoming confused by this tendency toward hugeness—you're not really sure you get to put the story of your great-uncle Bobby and his drinking too much, his being in the CIA, in this book or any book or how this may or may not be related to the history of sugarcane in the New World. Let's call the places your story will visit, in time, your novel's *temporal mapping*. Let's say this starts to sketch itself, that the territory will start to etch the boundaries and edges of the landforms of your story's hugeness, with the size and shape of your own feelings of insignificance giving the sheer size of our country's landscape.

Let's say defining its temporal mapping will become part of your quest in writing this book of yours.

Every good story is not only a quest, it is also its own encapsulated mystery. As you enter the House of Plot you need to make room for everything that comes to visit. You can't yet know what your book does and doesn't contain because its narrative future is not yet written. Story is as curious as you are about what its noticer is going to get to notice now that we've rigged the back of the building with its proper landings and windows, its fire escapes, and the truck, late model, equipped with a really magnificent sleeping compartment built right our over the hitch.

It's only by climbing all the way up here to the third floor, getting to Room 307, by looking down into the cab that we can start to get at the reasoning of the trucker Bob McGaw, that he's left the cab in park with the AC running because he has this new little dog. We see this dog now, as we gaze down from the upstairs window, how its nose is snizzling the side window, since he already loves Bob McGaw and really misses him, though they've only been a dog-and-man couple for a couple of hours.

And we have to pause to notice a few things about the man-dog couple, to see how well they do or do not go together, and we think, Huh? in that Bob McGaw is an *enormous* man, tall, big-boned, and gone to fat, and this dog's so small they look ridiculous in each other's company. Bob McGaw's gone in to buy drinks and snacks.

It's one of those really tiny, tiny dogs, like movie stars have, white and bug-eyed and shivery, and it has huge ears that look like they've been borrowed from a toy-store rabbit.

The dog's like plot—small, intense, self-confident. Characteristic of its breed, it is smarter than its owner. It is smarter than Bob McGaw in that it knows something the trucker cannot know until they're halfway across Ohio, when they stop at a rest stop. This is what Diego knows:

There's a girl hiding in the truck's sleeping chamber. Her sole possession? A potted red geranium. She is seventeen years old and she is barefoot.

⇒

YOUR STORY IS its own rare mystery, as your plot will now go out of its way to prove to you. You have no idea what it contains. You cannot yet know the Ending to your story, because it doesn't take place in Room 307, as you first intended, back when you thought it was going to be one of those neat books that concerned itself with politics in a minor way, did good things, had the right attitudes, wrapped itself right up.

Plot *hates* that kind of thing.

What plot says to us is *Hey, you?*—as in you and me—you don't actually know *the first thing* about what's going on in this story of yours. You aren't going to know anything either until you settle back and allow yourself to write it.

Its Ending, for instance? Its Ending doesn't yet exist. It will come in a form so well disguised, so cleverly hidden, it might as well be Halloween with Bob McGaw cross-dressed as the Queen of Hearts and Diego going as the March Hare.

You cannot *know* this Ending because it hasn't yet been written. It's still a room in a house, a room that you believed was the one at 14th and Webster, NW, but actually may lie two thousand miles away in a farmhouse in Nebraska.

Your novel's Beginning and its Ending both belong to the building that has not been built, in a place that has not been made, in a land that has not been named because in your pre-book Flat

Earth universe it is still an undiscovered continent that people think is India, so the New World doesn't even yet *hypothetically* exist.

This Ending is also the place your story sets out from, a place plot and story already know that that they are working together to hide from you. That an Ending and its Beginning are united is perhaps the oldest narrative truth, that we never recognize how they are always and relentlessly one until the instant that the drapes on the sleeping cabinet are thrown wide and the sleepy girl with the messy hair yawns and grins at the huge and truly *horrified* man, as the bright light of narrative recognition streams in and all this begins to *dawn on him*. What are they to each other? Who will they become? We cannot yet know, and plot's asking us to do this the hard way: by the long haul, by driving two thousand miles west to Nebraska with GPS furnished by the narrative demands of a *Chihuahua*.

Gigi, meanwhile, yawns and stretches and needs to use the bathroom.

4

The Mechanics of Narrative Time

There are three secrets to writing a novel.
Unfortunately, nobody knows what they are.

—W. SOMERSET MAUGHAM

WHAT MAUGHAM MEANS is that each novel contains its own three secrets and that the only way we're going to figure out what these are is to let these novels of ours write themselves. So our push has been to get language down on the page; to allow our books to develop naturally; to trust that as they've become more and more themselves, they will start to display their own structural elements.

This happens as our books start to indicate subtly how they'd like their temporal components to be organized, seeming to ask: *You're thinking this is After? Or does it still feel more Before?*

But After or Before *what*, exactly? We will answer that only through the writing of our books.

⮩

A NARRATIVE'S MECHANICS are most easily defined as its functional and technical parts. The language we use here describes the mechanical aspects of our craft. And we cannot make direct and immediate sense of this language until we have come far enough along in the process to get a hands-on feeling for how all of this will begin to work.

And maybe it's ironic that we'll need the work of our metaphoric hands in building these metaphoric structures, these houses made of different kinds time—before the abstract terms we meet can start to feel concrete enough to make sense to us. It's only by engaging in what will feel like manual labor that books stop being vague ideas and start to convince us of their ability to become *realized. To realize* a structure is what architects call getting a building they've designed actually built. For the best architects, it is said, the ratio of built to unbuilt is not even one in ten.

We need technical language to be able to discuss how the mechanical aspects do their work when they are working right; we need it to diagnose when they aren't. Structural problems are also the good news: Since they're structural, they're also elemental. Basic.

Basic, however, makes us feel like we're stupid, that we should already understand all this. But why should we? It's technical, after all. We are only now learning how to build these things.

What we will learn here (and in the short entries in Part Two) is the vocabulary that helps us articulate why a structure does work. We will come to understand the difference between, say, the narrative demands of a story's Beginning as opposed to those of its Middle. We'll also be able to talk about the *structural givens* of our craft. Those common elements of the longer narrative apply equally to all of us, and they include *After and Before*, *cause and effect*, and the six all-important elements we call *kaleidoscopic*, for the manner in which they act and interact: *time, tense, tone, person, point of view*, and *perspective*.

We need to know about the mechanics *in general* to appreciate our novel's structural quirkiness. To appreciate why, for instance, it will seem to be moving along so smoothly that you'll hardly notice its mechanisms at work—right before they very suddenly break down. Those horrible mechanical noises, those pings, clangs, and crashes? They are the sounds that the suspension of narrative disbelief makes as it hits the bottom of the Dumpster, as our novel announces, "Hello. And oh, by the way, I'm totally fake."

But it is here, as the structural elements come off the rails, that we tend to learn the most, another reason we won't become overly dismayed if our books haven't turned out to be perfect by the third or eleventh time we've rewritten them. This is all about *craftsmanship*, and this is good news, too, because craftsmanship is what I can teach and what you can learn.

Writing a good book involves craftsmanship to a degree that no one ever anticipates—it's in craft that these books start to act fleet and light and self-confident, as if they know what they are doing. This is where our books start to intimate that they may turn out to be really, *really* good, so good they'll be a shock to everyone, especially *you*.

It just so often takes this kind of stubborn and diligent effort to work your way up from apprentice to journeyman to master. Our novels, meanwhile, are teaching us technique, which is why we let them take all the wrong turns they want.

⇒

THE MECHANICS OF narrative time are those nuts-and-bolts, nonmystical elements that serve to hold these thirteen tons of narrative as all this sets off on what will immediately feel like a transcontinental journey. The structural mechanics equip the longer narrative with its only hope that the storytelling mechanism can successfully carry a novel's enormous narrative weight, for however far it needs to go.

The mechanics are the study of how fiction does what it does, achieves its effect. You know much of the terminology already. What you may not realize is the degree to which all structural elements are interdependent. That perspective, for example, establishes point of view, which then manages tone.

The most simple shift in time, tense, tone, or in person, perspective, point of view will bring subtle or dramatic changes to every other element. All storytelling aspects are similarly interrelated, subject to every twist of narrative change. Craft demands that we understand the subtle ways all the elements work together.

So you're learning that you can change them, that nothing among the moving tons of narrative is fixed and unchangeable, that you may want to begin in one tense or person, then shift to another, then shift back again. You begin to feel the effects of these changes, that a change to one of the kaleidoscopic elements brings change all down the line of the narrative.

You want to experiment, because that's how you will become adept at understanding and mastering how these elements make us feel. We call them the three *t*'s (time, tense, tone) and the three *p*'s (person, perspective, point of view). Nothing is more important to our books than what their combined efforts contribute. We need to know how all this works not just generally but specifically, to get at what your own novel needs exactly *now*.

This need asks the writer to come to his or her narrative project with a respect for its own complex and sophisticated interior clockwork. Time will not only be carefully calibrated by a book's mechanics but also hidden, telescoped, slowed down, vanished, or evaporated. Time can be brought by the interior mechanisms to meet itself, so the future and the past are conjoined, their systems intermixed.

Time belongs to place. Time also belongs to each character who comes alive over the course of the narrative (each character, that is, who doesn't turn out to be furniture). To time, the architecture of the novel says, attention must be paid. Nothing demands more serious consideration.

➤

THE MECHANICS REQUIRE that we fully apprehend the difference between a scene's narrator and its noticer, and how the two work together. We must also hear the difference between the voice of the author—our own intrusive voice—and that of the storyteller, which, we quickly learn, is always distinct from ours.

Narrative structure asks that we understand the complex temporal mechanisms defined by the novel's length, that we appreciate how crucial the matters of sequence and causation are to our book's ability to move directly and meaningfully from one scene to the next.

It is only by our paying close attention to the techniques of structural mechanics that these novels of ours will be able to acquire what they so earnestly strive for—a belief in their own reality. The longer story's conviction derives from the sense that the storytelling mechanism finally steps up to occupy a coherent narrative universe empowered and informed by its own set of natural laws.

Narrative mechanics will make the novel's world make sense. A story's plausibility can be measured by the same tests that structural engineers use in the real, 3-D world. A sound, thoughtfully made structure will stand and operate as it was meant to, while the one whose architecture and engineering have failed will either fall apart immediately or gradually collapse under its own weight.

This is what happens to any book that cannot get itself to feel fast and light.

It is the length of these narrative projects of ours—their density and weight—that risks their structural failure. Too many good books lie buried under the ruins of what they could never become. This means they could never become fast enough to take off, to defy their own gravity. For them—and for us, their makers—everything depends upon our growing skill at temporal engineering.

⇒

IN STUDYING THE mechanics and architecture of narrative time, we immediately happen upon the shape of the narrative triangle. All stories very naturally triangulate between two known elements and a third, hidden piece. This piece rides way ahead of the travelers on the lonely highway, or it follows along, headlights off, shadowing them.

The narrative takes on the unstable shape of the *sprung triangle*, one with two sides open at their hinge. This opening lets the narrative pull us forward, into the future of the story, riding upward along the storyline in the direction of *narrative expectation*.

The arc of the narrative is itself a sprung triangle, whose beginning and end always seek to reunite, to restore the shape, to reestablish structural stability and order. We've encountered this desire before: It's the one architects—psychologists as well— call closure. It is the kind of knowledge that comes to us in *feeling*. *We* also call this an *affective state* or name it *intuition* or *instinct*.

It is here where our bodies will go ahead to solve a story's riddles far in advance of our thinking minds. Our feeling states are so much quicker with the subliminal clues a story offers, and our intellects must work overtime to catch up. A novel's proper ending always *feels* as if it is perfectly placed, yet it feels surprising, too. We've stopped believing we will ever *get* there— then, very suddenly, we are there in the state of our own sense of *arrival*.

The past, present, and future in a narrative also triangulate, as do so many of the novel's active elements, from the most complicated to the most elemental. An active scene will *always* triangulate. It will move from its own present moment, propelled by an *active* past and pulled onward in the direction of its own *active* future.

In this three-part dynamic, time is often the invisible element; it doesn't immediately register. Time is needed, however, to activate an episode, to move it from a static *now* in the direction of *conflict, complication, change*. Time, in this construction, swings open on a *narrative hinge*, opening a story ever outward. Each cause begets an effect that then becomes another cause. These work along the line of the story, moving the narrative always in the direction of home, its final destination (see *ABCs*).

Our stories always organize themselves in this triangulating fashion. We can use the triangle as a diagnostic tool when we feel the mechanics of our story's time to have come apart. You will *feel* this happen, a sudden lostness: The story will either bog down because it's overloaded or stall because it's lacking its third element.

Whenever a story goes, the cause can always be traced to its angles or *vectors*, which are no longer moving along the arc of the narrative. They're heading somewhere but have lost their sense of *directionality*.

Remember that it is only natural that a story will always be actively working on its arrival at its next destination. It does this by the careful mechanisms of plot, which is always working toward meaning. We know we're on track with meaning when the vectors match, when they angle or point in the same anticipatory direction.

Our novels move in the way they do because they want to imitate life. The longer narrative mirrors our own perceptions of reality, in that we can know something about the past, something about our own present moment of existence, but the future must remain hidden from view. It lies beyond the hinge in time that marks the arc of the narrative; even when plot tells us what *will* happen, we cannot know what these events actually *mean* until we arrive at them.

In the Bob-and-Gigi story, to which we'll return in a moment, two dynamic narrative elements of more or less equal force hit the road with tons of narrative materials they're being forced to carry. Why must they haul this barge, tote this bale? Because their *difficulty* is what will make this a novel.

They will be easily identifiable as foils, allowing one to define another in the manner in which they're opposites: big, small, dark, light, a man, a girl, one young, one old, one deft, one slow.

They are also bonded by their unspoken need to go search for their missing third, which is . . . ?

This will often feel musical, in that the hidden instrument—a tuba, say—may play the same note every so often to remind us what we're looking for. Or the tuba may sound a theme or scattering of notes that is barely heard. This is the hidden part of the three-part chord that will play triumphantly at the story's end.

≥

THESE MECHANICS, THEN, teach us the basic geometry we need to build our houses of time. While higher math and physics may be interesting—especially in diagramming how a narrative works after the book is finished—we'll get a book written only by virtue of our manual labor.

This is to say that a novel's truths are best arrived at via the writer/reader's haptic, or bodily, knowledge of the world. Those are the feeling states that our bodies understand *before* our minds do. What happens when we allow the plot to dominate the story is that our novel's *thinking* is allowed to show.

This chapter articulates how the mechanical aspects of our craft work together to produce *the feeling states* that a book will spark. We share these feelings with our readers, which is how folks can agree about what a novel says. We work toward imparting a story that feels *true*.

These feeling states, as we remember, are the doors through which we enter the narrative. There are the three of them, as you recall: sympathy, empathy, and a correlation to our intuition about reality. We come back to them continually.

The ABCs will help with the run-through, what the builder calls a punch list: Do the characters inspire my *sympathy*? My *empathy*? Do the characters, the story, and the story's situation all *correlate to my intuition about reality*?

These are all tests of the truth.

So our intellects come into play only after we've been at this long enough to feel the story coming into its own by asserting its own triangulating nature. Your story knows the order of its own events, its own chronology. Now plot is telling us the order in which we are to *learn* of these events.

You'll be amazed at the degree to which your novel already knows about technique. It knows, for instance, what a *flashback* is, which we will discover later in this chapter, as soon as we can induce a character to have one.

⇛

FIRST WE LOCATE the story in its living scenes. To find the narrator you need only listen to the story, being keenly attentive to the voice in which it is whispering itself to you.

The one steadfast rule about the narrator? It is *never* you and me. We're called other things: *writer, author.* Why? We are not actually IN these books of ours. Even though there may be a nine-year-old who carries my name and DNA, who shares my birth certificate, whose life events exactly match my own life events, including dates and times on my parents' death certificates, as in the stories in my last book, I am *not this person*.

And this is why: The human being I am lives in the real world of time. You and I have been irrevocably changed by the alchemy of time, which is at work even now and so changes you and me further each and every day we are alive. This is why a memoir sits in the realm of storytelling right next to its best friend, fiction.

You and I are not the same people we were last week. This makes the person in the memoir our re-creation. We are simply not the same, emotionally, spiritually, physically—and this is good news, too, because it means we are still alive.

And it is *only* by allowing the story itself to speak that it will begin to reveal its truths.

⮞

TRUTH: IT TAKES root in your book the very moment that you let it. You will find truth most directly *in scene*. You set yourself down *in scene*. You allow your body to haptically inhabit the body of a character. You'll find that you come and go from your characters' bodies, sharing the haptic knowledge of the world whenever you give this character a moment of witness. Witness says this to be your noticer.

Here's what happens out back behind the rooming house when Gigi becomes the noticer. The scene starts in the second person, then migrates to third. It's set in present tense, which makes it feel quick, without time built in for reflection. This influences its tone, which is jaunty, which fits the character, who is an adolescent girl whose motto might be "What, me worry?"

You didn't know you got to mix second person with third, to flip back and forth between the two?

You need to become more like Gigi, who in this passage knows to the bottom of her soul that it's all a matter of what you can get away with:

> You've always been lawless, you realize, maybe addicted to the rush of feeling at-risk, which you get at by doing what your stepmother would call *wrong*. Wrong or right? You don't necessarily go by that.
>
> You just like the little jolt of adrenaline you get walking the blurry line where the rules go mute, which is how you feel as you find yourself in the alleyway back of the bodega, barefoot, your red geranium in hand, staring nose to nose with the little white dog that's wriggling all over itself. You know all you really have to do is act like you know what you're doing and you'll more than likely get away with anything.

Gigi has always been convinced that no one's really watching her, people are busy, her stepmother has a place to run, people to see. This stepmother's an important person and likely won't miss her when Gigi's gone.

No one is really paying attention, Gigi thinks, as she stares into the window of the dark red truck cab. She's hoisted herself up on the running board to be tall enough to see in, keys in the ignition, engine running; she's just figuring out that this is because of the little dog, because the trucker guy left it going so he could run the air conditioner, though its late afternoon and not that hot. The dog's acting completely spazzed out, so overjoyed to see you, Gigi thinks, that the two of them were already bonded, though this is not the kind of dog she'd ever imagine owning.

It's one of those prop dogs, actually, that Hollywood movie stars keep in their purses, stardom being a state of mind Gigi couldn't stand because she prefers feeling invisible. She can't stand being that kind of girl who needs to be looked at to feel real, her keeping her face all placid-smiling-tense as if she's ready to have her picture taken.

The dog's licking the window of the truck cab on the driver's side and making a little hurt noise, as if to say, "I've been waiting for you." You watch your hand impulsively open the door of the cab, and you swear to

God this is how it actually happened, as Gigi's thinking, though she can't quite imagine who she's telling this to if not her stepmother and its years later now and she's no longer in trouble.

The door opens. The dog springs into Gigi's arms; it never occurred to her to take him. The dog's just there, this crazy licking and wiggling thing, all bug-eyed and strange.

And she knows she needs to put the dog back before the trucker guy comes out, and she tries but she can't get it to SIT! STAY! or in any way behave. The moment she puts it down, the dog leaps back up at her, and now she's a little panicky, afraid she'll close its little chicken-bone-skinny legs in the door, so she is actually forced to hop up into the cab and close the door on herself. She puts the potted geranium down on the floor of the cab.

This is how the whole thing happened, Gigi thinks, that she then looked up and saw the big man coming around the side of the brick building in the rearview mirror, so she climbed over the potted plant and brought it with her as she went farther into the cab to hide, climbing the three rungs up to the bunk over top the fold-away dining table, the dog, with its glittering black eyes seems to say: Okay, I'm new here too, and I'm never going to tell on you.

This is how it happened, as Gigi will remember it later: that her fight with her stepmother was bad, but they'd have got over it, that they'd had worse and they'd both recovered, that it was an accident, that she never *intended* to run away.

⋍

TWO PERSONS, SEVERAL tenses, a dog who's a plot device. Our scenes do come to us as unbidden as dreams, showing that they're at work over in their own parallel universe while we pay them little attention.

They demonstrate that they understand the causality of the narrative universe, that the dog's being in the car caused Bob to leave the AC running, that the dog also caused Gigi to open the door so she could pet him.

We find the story in its scenes. They begin to reveal their order. And yes, this will take a draft or two. That's right, I said, *a draft or two*.

Your ability to bravely write your way through the *drafts* is the best predictor for whether or not your book's going to turn out to be any good. You will need to be tough-minded, with also, maybe, a constitutional stubbornness, a matter-of-fact dedication to the hard, day-after-day labor of writing a novel. A dedication, in fact, that is so much more important than *talent*.

Talent can so easily get in your way, as it makes you think this ought to be easy. It is never easy. In the real world, success-ful novels are being written *every single day* by those of us who might be most kindly described as ordinary.

Really. Completely ordinary people write good books. They do this in a perfectly competent fashion. They do it because they're driven to, because they get organized, because they try hard, because they study the form, because they've decided they have a story that's worth the time it will take them to write it.

Learning the elements of craft *enables* a person to get the story down coherently. You study in order to learn. You also then practice the same thing over and over again to get it down. You learn to treat narrative time respectfully by treating it as what it is, which is fictive mass. Its weight accumulates within a novel as the book grows, getting bigger and longer and more complexly involved.

⋑

THE PHYSICAL FEEL of narrative mass makes it resemble the live weight an architect must confront in creating a structure.

A novel's structure is like a building's in that it's made of solid materials that allow it to feel both spacious and comforting. It must feel empty enough to have room for us. This means we, the story's readers, have been considered, that a place has been made for us so we can step in and share the feeling of entering into a narrative that's progressing within these rooms of time (see *sequencing*).

A narrative must, therefore, have depth, length, width, a sense of a room's ceiling height—in the Peterbilt cab the ceiling height is seventy-five inches.

Some rooms are capacious, some dark as caves. The Peterbilt sleeper cab is cozy; it also has that new car smell. All rooms must, however, feel like they open outward along time's hinges, so we can see our way through this narrative moment and on to the next. This is an architectural precept: You must never enter into a structural dead zone or psychological cul-de-sac.

We need to be able to see the door and windows through which we can glimpse other narrative possibilities. It is through the window that we can see the activities of a subplot as they go hurtling by.

A novel requires a growing sense of its own narrative mass, that its meaning *accretes*, that the story grows in narrative *moment*. And a novel has many other houselike properties. It will develop a sense of its own history and will often seem to lie in the neighborhood of others that look like it, that help define it in context. Your book's neighborhood is its *genre*.

Each particular structure wants to feel *inhabited* in a way that's never happened before or since. It may well have its own ghosts—like any house that has been around for any time at all. It may creak and groan with its own imperfections, the manner in which it is canted just a smidgeon off the *plumb line*.

It is important that the novel *not* be perfectly symmetrical because nothing in the real world—the world we open our eyes to witness, the one we call nature—exactly matches side to side or front to back. A narrative will always, actually, be asymmetrical in a particularly predictive way. It's predictive in that it matches the orderly disordered feeling of nature (see the *fractal nature of the narrative*). This is a novel's regular irregularity.

So you write a draft to *let in* your novel's very natural imperfections, the way any family that actually lives there is *not like* any *other* family, either happy or unhappy, who *ever lived*. In writing this draft you begin to witness your longer narrative's sense of its own individuality, in terms of its momentum, its direction, its *will*.

This will is expressed as your story's voice. This is the novel's *narrator*. The tone will predictably change, as will perspective and point of view. In a scene, the noticer will be positioned in greater or lesser narrative proximity to the action depending on the effect you want to achieve.

At *every* structural hinge—these are those narrative junctures, those bends in time that allow us access to the story—we must imagine ourselves climbing up in the truck cab to reside within the sleeper cab of the narrative. We want that haptic surround-sound IMAX 3D experience. In fiction this works via the three *p*'s and the three *t*'s.

We are asking that our bodies be allowed to participate in this other world, that we find our own avatar to carry us there.

⇒

THE STRUCTURAL MECHANICS of the longer narrative and the natural laws the engineer or architect encounters match because our novels want to be believed in just as dreams want to be believed in. Novels want to impersonate real life, to be like life. And they must—or they'll fail to convince us that we need to leave our own time and place to explore their often more vivid, authentic, more realistic-seeming world. So many of us enter into the worlds of fiction in a quest for a more verifiable-feeling truth.

Our stories seem, therefore, to go by physical laws that lie down right next to the ones we already know, those regarding gravity and the forces that determine the movement of matter. So, yes, the roofbeams in our stories will be heavy; yes, they will be even predictably hard to raise.

And writing a book may take you about the same amount of time as it does to build a house. Having a long project that will need to transpire over time has its own advantages: As it goes along, it will become a measure of your capacity to stick to this often-thankless-feeling work. It will also continually teach you new things. Your novel will tell you things you never knew about your own soul, these being those truths known so far by no one else but you.

I love being inside the process. Writing a book works for me as living in one certain house probably does for more normal people, those less enmeshed in their other, hypothetical existences. Being swept away into the realm of the hypothetical is one of the occupational hazards of being a novelist.

The structural elements teach you their own mechanics— we're remembering that *mechanics* is the study of the way *action interacts with matter*. This is to say that there are moving parts of this project, which might be called "fiction," but that these must interface with the solidly material elements of an everyday existence already known to us.

A story taking place within its enlarging and ever more elaborated situation as it plays out over time is one definition of a novel.

So we encourage the novel to elaborate, to grow, to become complex, to start to feel *big enough to be round*, which means we get busy inventing everything that makes this world. It must become complex—woven, for instance, of the intricacies of plot/subplot—to achieve a sense of narrative gravity.

This sounds as if the longer narrative will also have many whims and desires, but these will feel *so much stronger* than mere passing impulses. These books of ours are developing, as they acquire narrative mass, a mechanical integrity in which they will begin to teach us how they'd like to operate, also what to keep and what to lose.

We learn this through the process of doing something only to do it again—and then again. The journey, for me, is an inheritance from my pioneer family, a tenacity of spirit, which is what it must have taken to walk behind an oxcart for two thousand miles to reach the Pacific Ocean.

My grandmother—who had a gallery and frame shop—would take a framing job apart again and again until she had done the job perfectly. I see the same tenacity of spirit in my son, who has taught himself how to rebuild a car by the complex but often-meditative practice of doing it.

I taught myself to be a novelist the same patient way, by allowing myself to be wrong and wrong and wrong again, forgiving myself for not being as easily gifted as a girl I knew in school named Pam O'Shannessey.

My greatest strength? I've always allowed myself be wrong for as long as it takes for me to learn the truth of what my book wants to say from the inside out. I let myself be wrong. I absolve myself ahead of time; I am forgiven all my lapses and failures.

In this I've discovered something profoundly comforting: that I'm happiest when I'm at work on a book. I simply feel most actively alive when I can walk through a novel's many rooms. A book, as I'm writing it, gives me someplace I always need to be and it feels to me like a home.

➤

IT'S IN THE novel's many rooms, however, its sheer, narrative hugeness, that we begin to get ourselves in trouble. Knowing exactly how structure is working doesn't matter so much to the writer of the shorter narrative. The writer of a short story is already grounded in specifics, the story's need to show its incidents and event. There's no time in a short story for its teller to go wandering off the storyline in pursuit of larger context. The short story writer has a finite, more or less manageable number of pages and scenes and characters. And a short story doesn't want to be big enough to be round. If it does, there's probably something fundamentally wrong with its trying to be a short story; it's more than likely a piece of a broken novel.

Our novels, however, need to be large, even all-encompassing. They sometimes need to go on and on, taking up volume after volume. They can become a life's work, a writer sitting down to the same story year after year—the way that James Joyce retells the same story of Dublin, 1904, over and over again, or Faulkner visits and revisits Yoknapatawpha County.

It's in this sheer magnitude, a novel's massiveness, the astonishing amount of *narrative territory*—in both time and place—that confuses us. Each character has his or her own *chronology*, each scene its own Before and After, its own Ending and Beginning, each event its cause.

As novelists we become those who work inclusively, who never met a theme we didn't want to go investigate. We *add in* instead of subtracting, trying to get to the realistic sense of a complete narrative *volume*.

With so many characters, storylines, intersecting plots, vectors marking the lines of action, and angled confrontations leading ever outward toward other revelations, it is no wonder we become confused. Every juncture and vector and angle sends us off in a missed direction.

This is why we rejoice in the purely mechanical aspect of the structural work, which gives us both tracking and GPS.

⇒

A NOVEL MAKES its own narrative map as it goes along—mapping means we can backtrack, trace our route, find out exactly where we took the wrong exit on the Interstate, also figure out why that particular off-ramp beckoned so compellingly. Structure is always the good news, because if it's structural, we can fix it.

Too bad we experience our novel's going wrong to mean we are not good people, that the lostness our book is making us feel is so basic that we feel sick and discouraged. Lostness in a novel so often takes on a depressingly spiritual component, as if we are these pompous, self-deluded, and, above all, *untalented* hacks. If we can only allow ourselves to treat these early drafts as voyages of discovery, we'll stop being *judgmental* about the structural problems that are certain to present themselves.

Structural problems simply *always* arise. There's no help for it. The true test of the novelist is whether or not you allow them to defeat you.

⇒

ALMOST EVERY FALSE start or wrong-way run down an alleyway derives from a purely technical narrative mechanic that's somehow gone awry. We become befuddled by the Larger Thing. It is always this:

Why are we here?

Just when we thought we were about to get somewhere, we suddenly find ourselves lost in a windy hallway. *Lost in a windy hallway (because I am not a good person)* is how I almost always feel when my writing becomes diffuse and vague to itself.

It goes like this: The dream dims, we feel anxious, we realize we do not know where we are, since we're lost in the province of The Vagues. You realize you have *no idea* where you are in time or place or how you might have come here.

This means that we've lost track of our characters, that we've come off the angle of the narrative, that we are wandering out in the desert for forty days and nights. What it means is you need to go find your characters in their next active situation.

So we go find our story *in scene*. We'll take Bob's point of view this time—Bob's interesting in that his perspective is disadvantaged, in that he cannot know what he doesn't know. This energizes the story because it adds narrative irony.

He can know only whatever his physical person has him experience, that he's a big man who's also wearing another kind of weight: He is just emerging from the active grief over his wife's death, ten months earlier.

He's an inquisitive man, but he feels dull, as if he doesn't have a clue. And he truly doesn't. He has no idea about his immediate situation, that he has a minor child aboard his cab, that he's crossed state lines with her, that she's put her red geranium down in the sink of the kitchenette and has climbed up to the top bunk, where she has fallen asleep.

In the rig, however, from Bob's perspective, Gigi is hidden from the narrator's point of view, and we can know only what he knows.

Two hours out of Washington, headed west-northwest up Route 70 toward Route 80, through the Appalachians that give way to the Alleghenies, past the off-ramp for the town that calls itself Halfway, Maryland, and he's forced to wonder, *Halfway between what and what?* Here with the highway running diagonally across Pennsylvania in the map in his mind and this being coal country, all these ridge-backed hills with their narrow, somber valleys. Scots-Irish settled here, a dour race of hardscrabble people, as Bob knows since he's one of them.

The big and very powerful engine is pulling the rig laden with thirteen tons of household items, this one man's library, as Bob's been told, so he's hauling the burden of all this knowledge, the whole weight of the world, it feels, all the way across the country, and how anyone would find the time to read *thirteen tons of books* will remain a puzzlement.

Out the windshield not yet yellowed with bug-splat the Allegheny Plateau stretches out before him. He's crossed over it time and again, but the grandeur always moves him. He has the little dog asleep in his lap, he thumbs one of the tiny velvet ears, and tears suddenly ache in the back of his throat.

It's sunset, the colors being so streaky, the light so triumphant and beautiful and that he's got this dog to care for, which will give him purpose. He's startled by how he is so easily moved, brought to the verge of tears several times a day and not just when he thinks of her.

He calls her *her* in his mind because he can't yet bear to hear her name.

Since her death he's sold their house, put the money into trust for his grandkids' education, and invested in this cab, which cost $57,997, in Woodbridge, Virginia. He loves its deep blackish red, with its very subtle metallic flake, the power of its mighty engine, that it still has that new car smell, and that it's like a house on wheels for The Big Guy, as they call him at the service centers he'll come upon, that he and the dog will be happy here.

He thinks then that he hears his wife's voice scolding him: *Wesley Earl, you are one sentimental fool.*

So we get lost in the narrative trance and can find our way back only by inhabiting the three hundred pounds of muscle and gut that is Bob McGaw, whose real name—as we're discovering—isn't Bob at all, but Wesley Earl McGaw!

How do we know this? Bob himself just told us so.

⮑

WE HAVE JUST imported background, the story ranging backward as it sets out moving into the future.

Background is one of the trickiest of narrative mechanics: It becomes heavy so quickly, and these stories of ours will need to be calibrated to feel fast and light no matter how much we're asking them to carry.

The only way to import background is to make it an active piece of the story as it moves along, in that Bob can actively and realistically think of these things: wife's death, selling the house, kids being grown and gone. All of this is realistic, in that the thoughts don't take too long.

On this journey we want the cargo of the architect's live weight, those characters, scenes and situations that move the story along. Memories too. We want background to step up and become an active element, which means it does its work in the story's present time. Anything solid and set and past tense can no longer be brought into the storyline in active *confrontation*. And so we are now deciding where the storyline's rooms of time will actually stand. This structure is the hardest thing to get right the first time through—like trying to build a sandcastle with water and no sand.

What we can't yet understand is that the book itself evolves to the point where it seems to have its own godlike mind, which then decides how it will have time be parceled out and organized. The book's mind already knows its own start and finish, what leads to what, which event will logically trigger the story's next revelation.

A book finally knows itself, knows the order in which it would like to be told, which will feel like its events exist for the story to then come upon, so its structure feels discovered, as if its being unearthed from wherever we keep the larger narrative truth.

It will feel like this book isn't so much writing these truths as it is remembering them.

⮑

AND ANY DISCUSSION of narrative order now brings us to the flashback, which is a narrative element that is tricky, in that it's technical. Let me show you what I mean:

> Gigi is sitting in the driver's side with the dog in her lap. She isn't really seventeen, she is, in fact, turning fifteen and small for her age—she doesn't know how to drive. She must reach forward to place her hands at ten and two on the steering wheel, which lies out flat and is oversized. She's imagining she could probably drive this thing.
>
> And she is suddenly back on Cape Cod, or whatever that dune-ish place they used to go when her father was still alive was called, where they'd gone to spend a holiday.

She's maybe two or three; she's sitting in his lap as he's driving a dune buggy with half-flat tires out over the sand, and he's laughing as they bump along, his laugh coming out eruptive in bursts as the truck pitches and rocks, and she's laughing too but with that tight clutched feeling in the bottom of her stomach because she's scared.

This scene contains the flashback's trigger, which is its antecedent action, Gigi's putting her hands on the steering wheel. The trigger prompts the act of memory, which then presents as its own scene as a thought action. A flashback always belongs to the mind of a character and not to the mind of the book, in the same way time in a scene belongs to someone and not just to anyone.

It isn't an impacted memory in that there's nothing left in the remembered scene for us to go after. Nor is it embedded, because we don't return to the scene in which it has been placed.

⊃

THESE TECHNICAL PARTS feel hard only because we're not good at them yet. Your story is also probably being childish—mine almost always are—which means it seems to want, as we've mentioned before, to defeat you. Who knows why this happens. Stories simply like to show up with their clothes on inside out and backward, so the labels show. Maybe it makes them feel important, cool, original.

A story is so often like this, the sock turned inside out, exactly showing what plot must then work to hide. It is simply too hard—at least for me—to get all this right the first time through. In law, this is called discovery. All we're asking is that plot and story work together to begin to make a little bit of narrative sense.

The mechanical aspect of this process deals with the design and construction of something transcendent of its own structure, that splendidly individual thing that allows us to stand back and witness something that becomes more than a sum of its parts.

We simply honor the balancing imbalances of the triangulated, narrative threes. Threes are dynamic in a way a four-sided structure isn't, that a cause will prompt an effect that then becomes the narrative's next cause.

In the logic-based and causal universe we are here elaborating, every part of the narrative is finally related to the mechanisms of after and before, in that each domino stands somewhere in relationship to all other dominos taking part in the domino race.

So we witness the manner in which the narrative employs the sprung triangle, the way two elements will be asked to stand in opposition to the third. Every good book finds its own way to balance its own triptych of storytelling elements, the most important of which is buried in the *E* of the Ending, an *E* that also stands for narrative expectation.

The narrative rises in the anticipatory direction because the beginning must find its end, because all action works toward this expectation. The longer narrative is poised in the sprung triangle of expectation, knowing that all its questions want to be answered, the mysteries will be allowed to solve themselves, and we will move from a state of ignorance into one of knowing.

This is what a novel is: plot + story + the time it takes to work back toward stability and realization, toward knowing all the secrets that this story is going to give us in this particular version.

The story, its plot, all reduced and simplified, is allowed to elaborate over the magic of time.

⇒

WE ARE ALL delivered to a novel's Ending through its triangulation, wherein the narrative past moves into and through the present moment on its way toward the narrative future, following the arrows of time. This allows us to look back through the transparency of time's rooms that narrative mechanics affords us. It is hindsight that gives us knowledge and perspective. Time allows us to walk around a narrative event, to view it from all the various points of view.

We can see it in the present, in the immediate past that is still unfolding, in a past that has been completed—this called the past that has been *perfected.*

A novel has this sense, once we've finished it, of a time that has been perfected, in that everything in it becomes understandable, and it's here we very clearly see the mind of the book at work.

We can witness the entire narrative process making its way upward, drawn along by expectation, which says that the future can be *apprehended* and made tangible in a way we never can in the mundane reality of the day-to-day, where so much necessarily eludes us.

Its narrative mechanics make the novel its own closed system, one that allows for all elements and events to be united by utility, in the way they work together toward one aim, which is the story's ending. Real life is never so beautifully logical.

The narrative mechanics allow a novel's actions to be seen from all sides, including the three-dimensionality that their moving through time provides. This mechanism is called *parallax information*, which allows for an event, a character, a story's situation to be observed *evolving*—this is essential to the longer narrative because it delivers us to the novel's most important subject, which is *change over time*.

The mechanics allow time in the novel to keep progressing—this is how time delivers narrative change. Time moves along the arc drawn upward in the expectation that knowledge will be gained, which is where story gets its imperative. The knowledge is always one form of the same old story, which might be paraphrased *everything is different now*. This matches the other part of the same old story, which says, *It is also just the same*, as story settles back into order and stability out of the chaotic realm of *possibility*.

You must arrive at the Ending in order to know what a story means. This is called the *inevitability of retrospect*, or IOR (see *antecedent action*). IOR says the plot and story have worked together successfully to hide their mutual Ending behind the narrative hinge at the top of the arc of story, which is marked C (for *crisis, conflict, complication, climax, change*). It is the expectation of the longer narrative that it works toward—if not knowledge or wisdom per se, then at least *clarity*.

It also means that time's mechanics, those bringers of change, are working to replace everything broken, to put everything back the way it was found. This is how the novel is most vehemently *not like life*, which works in the direction of a future that may well have the less-than-successful outcome. In life we grow old, we die, our loved ones move away, the machine breaks down and cannot be fixed. When this happens in a story it's called narrative *entropy* or *randomness*.

The narrative's proper future is not only order—it is not only *in* order—it is an orderly system that is understandable to us. Narrative mechanics allow a story to make sense not only to us, the story's elements will make sense to themselves; the IOR is that sense of closing a book both completely surprised and thinking, *I knew it!*

The signs were there all along. Yet—and satisfyingly—we've been tricked.

⋑

NOW WE HAVE all the parts to this thing, this Gigi/Bob story: the vehicle ready to cover vast narrative distances, and the two (or three) protagonists, each of whom is sympathetic. We feel for them; we also feel with them, as each radiates an ache with which we resonate, which is their incompleteness, their sense of loss.

Each of them is an unstable element. Plot goes to a great deal of work to have these unstable elements meet in a *coincidence* that, in a novel, is always carefully plotted. Plot messes with the signage. Story says that we're headed northwest on I-70, crossing Pennsylvania's coal country, where the 70 is marked with signs spelled out in those plastic reflectors that light up only when your headlights hit them.

It's May 2005, the signs have been recently redone in a bold new face, a font designed specifically for this purpose. The highway department calls this font Clearview, in that its letters and numerals stand far enough apart that they won't halo and blur together.

Plot has selected Clearview to mark the important exits and interchanges, but has also cleverly tweaked the headlights on Bob's truck cab to flatten so the road signs will not light up. Bob's also maybe forgotten his glasses, so he's not reading as well as he should. He's singing along to the Drive-By Truckers, which he's got on his new iPod wired to the AUX of the brand-new, very beautiful machine that is his Peterbuilt. Diego rides along in his lap. Bob's headed out onto the Alleghany Plateau where he thinks some things about coal mining.

So for another little second we allow Bob to miss the signs and sail along in ignorance: He cannot read the signs. It isn't dark yet, he's forgotten his glasses, he's just like the rest of us, he doesn't yet know what he doesn't know, and the signs that we see but he cannot read have fallen away—because of plot's calibrations—into invisibility.

The narrative mechanics of IOR are the true test of plot, the blur on the Interstate sign that suddenly snaps into focus saying, Hey, Bob, hate to interrupt but you really are going to need to get this rig off the interstate *right about now*.

Plot says: I mean it, the stakes are high. We realize you're innocent of any wrongdoing but you do have *a minor child on board*! and you cannot even know how minor she is, since this girl is going to lie her way up one side and down the other, lie so convincingly you will not know *what* to believe, but you've already crossed state lines, which means you're really in trouble.

Sure, plot says, you did nothing wrong, Big Guy, nothing at all to deserve this fate, but then we *never* deserve our fates—just ask Shakespeare and the Greeks. So you'd better get this rig off the road right now and turn around because these days and with all that goes on no one is going to believe you!

Plot is the gear called reverse. Plot works through narrative mechanics to flip the switch on the story so you can watch your novel perform itself just as perfectly backward.

And yes, plot as a domino race may well feel mechanical when you look at it that way, that *this* caused exactly *this* to happen. Still, there is nothing at all wrong with the narrative machine that does *exactly* what we ask it to, which is to keep the storytelling suspenseful by doling out one complication after another.

Plot works through the sprung triangulated impulse of the scene in which complication is met, conflict worked through, so the story can move on to its next crisis. Plot makes these unpredictable. Your story is the agent of surprise. For our narrative purposes we've named the story Gigi. It is important that Bob and Gigi meet.

Why? because the gods of narrative seem to will it. Without Gigi, Bob's cross-country trek is just another meditation on life and time. Sure, sure, his truck cab's new and he's a great guy and all, but without her in his life he isn't interesting because he's been given no *dilemma*.

We need Gigi to import the unpredictable. Without surprise, your book goes dead. Story, too, is unpredictable and unreliable: It is always written from *this* point of view or perspective, by *this* narrator and we—as modern people—know that no one person has the complete truth of any given situation.

We are interested in a novel's many levels of truth, any version can be supplemented or contradicted by dialing the kaleidoscope of person, point of view, perspective, time, tense, tone.

We learn the various truths by virtue of what we call narrative *agency*: A character speaks aloud or we overhear their thoughts, but a character must earn our trust. A novel makes room for minds to be changed, for a good person to be turned to misguided pursuits, for an evil one to be redeemed.

We may need everyone's version, everybody's witness. What Gigi tells Bob about her past may turn out to be inadmissible in a court of law. We will not necessarily believe Gigi's testimony, who may well tell Bob, as they go along, the most shocking stories of what she's been through.

We don't need to believe her. We need only hear what she says, and we'll be able to judge for ourselves, through clues given us by the noticer. So plot will ask story the patient, rational, Bob-like questions that help a story straighten itself out: *Where do you come from? Who is currently missing you? Can you think where you may have left your shoes?*

Plot has the property of grinding down, trimming away the flash to get at the logical. It's plot that runs a time check. You learn that there may be nothing better to help alleviate the lost-in-the-funhouse feeling that comes with writing a novel than running a time check—you do it over and over again.

Story feels like happenstance: It's fitful, childish, organic. Plot, meanwhile, has that pleasant *real life* sense to it, that says reality is knowable. Plot feels fully formed, rationally adult, quantifiable—but inexpert hands can turn it wooden. When not enough accident is allowed into your book, it will feel deterministic and old-fashioned.

This is why you're going to have to let your story confound the plot, stand up, say whatever is on its mind, tease it, poke it in the gut. Story dances off, hides in the bathroom at the truck stop, and says it won't come out. Story makes fun of plot by diving out the window the moment plot thought it had its hands on it.

Story is evanescent. Plot, when given primacy over story, will weigh too much, can rob characters of vitality. When plot sits on story, story's never a match.

When plot wins, we have the novel that *ought* to work but it just doesn't. It goes by the rules, is lawful, predictably surprising. But it's also leaden, unreadable because it's deterministic. It does not feel real.

The mechanics are how we keep the two all-important elements in balance and alignment.

➤

PLOT. STORY. THE third element of the sprung triangle of the longer narrative is always Time, as an active element, Time, the bringer-on of change.

Bob will be changed by the actions of the novel on which he is embarked. The agent of change will come to him as Gigi, who will, in turn, be changed by her interaction with Bob over the time they are together.

The real reason people like you and me take the time to read and write these books of ours is to be present as this happens, witnesses to the wonderment.

We become ever more familiar with time working as an agent of change. Time settles in, becomes palpable, sifts down into the narrative so it can begin to hold its own shape. This lends it a sense of believability.

And time will want to feel believable. The narrative mechanics of a scene ask that time be respected, that those incidents and events that are written into a scene can plausibly take place in such a way, given the obvious rules of time.

Time seems to predate the characters' journey together. A character, in coming to life, will have its own accurate and personal chronology. A place owns its own time, even the Peterbilt truck cab is new in 2005, which sets it down in within the matrix of its own believability.

Time wants to take over and rule the longer narrative. It will seem to be keeping time, which expresses itself in lulls, pauses, rushes, and other elements we call *pacing*.

The mechanics of plot must, however, stay largely hidden in order for us to be allowed to participate in the story's narrative dream. We'll get back to the dream by finding Bob and Gigi steaming along the interstate in the Peterbuilt cab.

⇒

BURYING THE MECHANICAL apparatus means hiding the working parts before the structural walls go up. We sweep up after plot, vanishing its traces.

The walls are whatever we use to segregate the rooms into useful sections. A narrative is organized according to time. It may want to cluster according to its own system of narrative mapping. One common kind of temporal organization is *chapters.*

Chapters need to come only now that we're *later along* in the process, after we've come far enough that we know which room of time might need to stand next to which other room of time. Chapters are part of the final organizational pass that makes a manuscript into the book it will finally become.

We want these walls to vanish our novel's quiet plotting and thinking, to pretend that the house we've built of plot and story over time is a real thing that has always simply existed. We don't want it to show the work of our all-too-human hands.

A novel, nearly done, will suddenly stop being able to accept the one more thing you feel you need to add.

Eudora Welty had a name for this realization, this finishing, this sense of something's going off to be published: *the letter sent.* For me, it has always felt like a giant helium-filled apparatus that floats away, carrying me with it. I have the most joyful feeling that I am not longer responsible for remembering all the elements that have gone into it.

I don't have to remember all this, since the mind of the book now has that responsibility.

The mechanics of narrative *economy* are what make the novel its own right size, which can honestly be as large as it needs to be in order to adequately say whatever it needs to say.

A novel's world is always a better one than the one we live in, in that it is finally more coherent and logical. It is also maybe the only place people like you and me—that is, *novelists*—feel that we have control.

In order for your plot to work, you'll need to develop your own technical abilities as a writer. Technical ability is gained one way only, by the day-in-day-out practice of writing. We must learn the mechanical aspects of working with narrative time. This is nothing but demanding.

You may want to write an entire draft devoted to experiments with time. You may write the story in present, change it then to past. You discover you need another viewpoint. You write, you then take what's good and throw the rest away. You may write an entire draft only to find you need to throw it all away. That's right, you throw your writing *away*, good writing out with the bad.

This is your book teaching you how provisional a provisional draft really is, that you throw good writing out with the bad but it will not matter.

Know why? If it's any good it's true and if it's true it will always, always come back to you.

⊜

DAYS, WEEKS, MONTHS will go into your learning to act as if you are writing a novel. It's then—after a good long while—that you'll begin making these astonishing narrative discoveries. Your story's own story—in its deepest, largest, most true and profound sense—will suddenly be up and running, feeling like a living thing. Your novel suddenly seems to have autonomy. It may suddenly seem like it is writing you.

It will spontaneously begin making its own narrative discoveries: that the girl you're writing about rides westward because it is the future, while your story says the truck contains an entire dark continent of the past.

And we thought Bob was in the driver's seat but now—according to the laws of narrative mechanics—we're guessing that it must be Gigi.

⇒

AND THE STORY'S form will suddenly become manifest: You'll no longer feel bound to the sameness and regularity of these long sectional-feeling things, with which you have—up till now—been working. The story now shows you that a scene can be totally short, accomplished in, say, a line or two.

The trucker's driven the cross-country route so many times he has routine stops, but he's never done it with a dog before. He pulls up in a rest stop in Ohio to let the dog run. It's a warm night, late spring. Across the way new corn stands a foot high in fields that belong to agribusiness, Bob knows, monitored by satellite. These are what's known as "scattered acres."

He's gotten his body down out of the cab having gathered the little dog up in his large embrace, when he sees the girl standing in the shadows of the sleeper, back by the kitchen sink. She's holding a red flower in a brick-colored pot. She comes forward into the light. She has that messed-up look his own daughter once affected, her hair all which way, her eyes smeared with makeup.

Her fingernails are bitten and she's been working away at the polish, which is black.

"Now where the bejesus did you come from?" Bob asks.

"I snuck into your truck back in D.C.," she says. "Sorry. These people are after me, see? And they're like really violent criminals and I just had to get out of there."

"You expect me to believe that?"

"No," she says. "I guess not."

"You're a runaway?"

"I guess," she says. "Though no one's probably looking very hard. My dad died last year. He was a cop. Line of duty. My stepmother isn't really handling it."

"Where do you imagine you're going?" he asks.

"Grand Island, Nebraska," she says.

"Why?" he says. "You have people there?"

"Not really," she says. "I just kind of like the sound of it."

"How old are you?"

"I'll turn eighteen next month."

Gigi believes she can hear him thinking it over, weighing the costs and the benefits.

"Please don't turn me in, please don't let them send me back. I only have a few weeks to go until I'm legal, I want to get a job, I need to get away from her, she's mean as a snake, no kidding. I want to move out and be on my own. I get money from my dad's thing, you know, pension, whatever. I'm not like poor or anything."

He's a kind-looking man who looks a little ridiculous holding the tiny dog. His face is shadowed by some kind of sorrow.

I can do something here, the girl thinks. She sees him looking at her clothes, a tank top, cutoffs, her bare feet, which are dirty.

"I took off kind of spur of the moment," she says. "Please?"

⇒

THE NATURAL LAWS of our narrative universes, of Gigi's and Bob's, lie right beside that of the physical world we really do inhabit. Our worlds will match, by narrative parallax, those of the real world—or the story will not engage us.

The job of the novel is to create a fictional world so real that it seems to be giving us convincing information: that corn is a grass that, in late May in Ohio, might well be about a foot high.

The natural laws apply to all physical objects equally. This is why human beings can't convincingly fly in a story unless you've gone to the hard work to convince us that they can. A narrative world wants to feel logical. If your characters are going to fly, you will have to work to invent the wing suit that conforms to the physics of your realm.

Narrative information—the mass of a story, its pages and characters and scenes—conforms to the laws of the natural world. Our books, however, risk becoming overloaded with this information. What the novelist does—to avoid getting lost in The Information—is to get back to the most basic element, which is scene. You retreat always to episode, go there to look in at the narrative mechanics. In the episode we reconnect with the story, which is now steaming west on Route 80 through Iowa. It's now the next day. Gigi is still aboard.

What I just did is called a *time check*. You ask your story where its characters are—and it is actually true that they really do always need to actually be somewhere, even if we don't have our eyes on them. The story must know where its characters are. If your story doesn't know, you'll need to check back into the nap institute to dream them up again.

⇒

THESE MYSTERIES ARE accessed only by entering into the private narrative spaces of your own built universe—and usually not by going in the front way, which is often boring, being usual, but by climbing up its fire escape to the third floor to figure out who's at home.

The mysteries have to do with art, which is born of *magic* and *prophecy*. Art isn't the reason we write a novel, which is always the more workaday, truck driver–like, gut-and-muscle project—and what it takes to trundle thirteen tons of Western Civilization all across the country.

All this conspires. It sometimes begins to turn into art. This happens occasionally. It often seems to have little to do with you or me. A story simply happens, and when it does, it's almost always the result of a lucky accident.

You'll always think of it as a lucky accident, that his cab still had that new car smell, that it wasn't the crappy mess you'd have assumed a truck cab would have to be, this from your basic snobbishness and superiority bequeathed to you by your rich-girl mom, whom you barely knew, that a trucker would have a kind of junkheap existence.

You didn't know the first thing about truckers but assumed they'd all be called Bubba, the kind of person you'd have instinctively hated, who'd have taken one look at you, with your hair bleached white and sticking up with gel and the piercing in your brow, and thought you were worthless.

You're just surprised to have found a friend in the package this one came in, whom you first thought was your own opposite, in that you may be a lot of things, high school dropout, troublemaker, incident shoplifter, ardent pot-smoker, but at least you aren't what this guy is, which is hugely *fat* and a *man* and *old*.

So it's always seemed almost like a fairy tale, that you hopped into the cab of the Peterbilt truck with a seventy-five-inch cab, so new it still had dealer tags, and you plopped your red geranium down in the sink to give it a drink and that you felt not criminal but more like Goldilocks, who has found the place that feels just right, the one that feels like home.

⇒

STORY EXISTS *IN SCENE*, which is our refuge. So we're OK now, because we've found the place from where the story of Bob and Gigi will set out, and please note that it has taken us nearly 150 pages to get here.

Plot is the engine that's going to propel this entire narrative process in its quest, which is what makes it drive all night, covering vast amounts of narrative territory, a sprung triangle.

Mechanics dictate that a scene remain minutely focused: *Chihuahua, potted red geranium, girl who's fallen asleep*. Plot is the story's situation as enacted by the two of them, who rhyme in ways we are only now discovering: that each feels orphaned, alone, and lost.

Plot uses your characters as its props. It may sound hard-hearted, but we do *use* our characters. We use them, in fact, to enact the story, which is why they remain subservient to the story, in that the actions that they engage in existentially decree whether they are good, bad, funny, nice—which is why you need to always *show us* how they act instead of telling us about the content of their character:

> Bob's not asleep on the bottom bunk. Bob may never sleep again. Bob's imagining some cop grilling him, a highway patrolman asking over again and over again how it is he came to be traveling cross-country with this *minor child who in no way belongs to him*.

WHAT TIME TEACHES us is precision with which we'll be able to calibrate plot and subplot interactions. We also learn the names of the kinds of time that are available to us. As light slips away over the Allegheny Plateau we call it *ambient time*; it feels soft and glowy.

It's like Light-in-August time, the sense that we've connected with A Larger Feeling for the world, that this story belongs to time that spools forward, that gets its way.

We use ambient time to slip in and out of scene, to enter and exit chapters and sections, to get the wide narrative view that seems to be able to witness the curvature of the earth and says time's eternal and there will *always be* these barefoot girls walking down the road on their way to who knows where. It is from ambient time that we build narrative pauses and bridges.

OUR NOVELS TEACH their own three kinds of language. This is to tell us that every word in the body of a novel will belong to someone, and not to you and me. We're the writers, the authors. As authors we get to sign books, do readings, at which our main job—as my own dear editor reminds me—is to show up on time and not be a pain in the ass.

All language the book owns belongs to one of these three narrative functions: (1) The voice of the narrator (or narrators), who is easily identified because this is the storyteller, (2) The characters, (3) The Outside World.

But this isn't the *real* Outside World, instead it is our own as-realistic-as-possible version of the world, one that hopes to become a real seventy-five-inch Peterbilt truck cab, which Bob—whose name isn't really Bob, by the way—has only recently picked up from the dealer in Woodbridge, Virginia, on his way in. He's a contract employee, driving for J&K Moving.

This seems real enough because we do want to give it all this realistic detail. The language J&K MOVING, which the girl reads on the door of the cab, is real, imported from the Outside World. So are the voices coming out of the radio in Gigi's room, which—according to the rules of the narrative mechanics of time—can play only music actually invented on or before May 28, 2005, as that is the actual here and now in which this scene in taking place.

The word *Coke*—its letters formed in the mold into which the glass was poured as it was being made in Mexico—belongs to the Outside World, as do these words: *Hecho en Mexico.*

This language has been checked through customs, entered the airlock, arrived in the universe of your novel by the same process by which we use our own physical bodies to animate a story's sensations. We imagine the process of our own climbing the fire escape and jimmying a window in order *to enter* the story, and, man, these garden walls are high and hard to climb.

We import this language by dreaming it into the narrative process whereby the storyteller then begins to say it.

➠

IT TAKES A lot of work to get the part about climbing up and down and in and out of the windows of a scene just right. It takes the physical effort of reimagining.

And we do need their honest-to-god bodily sensations to get our characters to come to life. Our stories ask us to convincingly inhabit characters who are not you and me: a seventeen-year-old girl who weighs less than a hundred pounds, a fifty-four-year-old man whose weight hovers around three hundred.

Bob is, however, a very beautiful man. He's a careful dresser, who has his shirts washed and pressed professionally. When dancing, he's light on his feet. We need to understand the sensations of being in this other body because it is through that craft that we climb through the window of the narrative and enter the story.

⊃

You climb up into the cab of the story, and the place immediately begins to exhibit the prehensile feel you want from it, that it's alive and it has its mitts on you. You become subject to your own story's gravity. This is sometimes hard to escape from.

It has always been harder for me to pull myself up and out of the narrative world than it is for me to enter it. Put another way: I fall into the dream easily, and it's hard for me to awaken.

I have learned to use this ability to write when I don't really seem to be writing. I dream the dream of the story when I'm driving a carpool or listening to something that doesn't really interest me.

I'm like those people who can sleep with their eyes open.

I wrote my first book sitting on the toilet with its lid down, with one then the other of my small children in the tub. This is exaggeration, of course. I exaggerate because I'm a fiction writer. But it is also true that I wrote that book folding laundry, while shopping, driving, stirring the soup, carrying on with my normal day-to-day.

I learned in writing that book how to live like a novelist, which is day-in-day-out and often surreptitiously. You write *all the time*, writing whether you seem to be doing it or not. It's like prayer. It comforts you. It becomes a spiritual practice.

So it is for most writers I know: we're the long-haul truckers, all but addicted to distances. This is a happy state of mind for us, our way of being spiritually healthy. We've learned that we are best integrated as individuals when we are living in the manner characterized by Flannery O'Connor as "the habit of art."

The habit of art: This means you begin to *experience* the world in a entirely a different way. You begin seeing, hearing, living, breathing, thinking as a storyteller does, witnessing life with the deeply involved yet passionate detachment that allows you to think in the case of almost any extremity, stopping the car to ask: *I wonder what narrative use I can make of this?*

Writing something as large as a novel requires that you get up *every day* and reinvent not only yourself as the person writing *this* novel, but also the job you're doing, a reasonable facsimile of a fictional wheel.

Night and day, while sleeping or half awake, you now let your mind live the rhythms defined by the line on the highway driving west, those mile markers that prove this story is *going* somewhere. You are getting someplace: *This*, you think, *is becoming interesting.*

So it matters little that you can't spend eight hours a day sitting at your desk—so few people have that kind of time. The story comes alive in your mind, you take it along with you where you go, you practice. It becomes your rod and your staff.

Our aim is simple: We're trying to keep our stories alive in our minds by listening to them tell themselves every single day. You write whenever you can. You write day in, day out, for weeks, for months, on end. You do it in traffic, while half listening to some not very interesting friend complain about the very same things she's always complaining about, knowing you'll hear her when she comes to anything new and interesting.

So you give yourself over to the story. You abandon the grand ideas you have about the shape it ought to take and allow the story to shape itself. In architecture the process is called drafting an elevation. In writing a novel we call it shaping the narrative materials. We do this by plotting the arc of the story. For our ascent up the outside of the building that has its window on the third floor we use what we call the *ladder of complication.*

⇒

WE USE A critical vocabulary because it teaches us to think about our novels diagnostically when something goes wrong. Something will go wrong. What this is will almost inevitably be structural.

Something isn't right; scenes don't match. In the movies this concern is called *continuity*. You need to shoot it differently, to back up, come back at this a different way, so you do a time check, you look at tense, tone, perspective, which is the width and depth of the scene, the lens through which you're viewing it. You check person, that is: first second third. Where is the narrator in terms of point of view, distant or far away?

You learn to change the three *t*'s, change the three *p*'s; you listen; you reevaluate. You look at what you're asking of all those myriad devices we use to try to enter the Lost World of the Past. You learn to be specific about *memory* and what it really means, as there are different types and kinds.

You look deeply at your noticer; is your noticer neutral and dispassionate, or are you, the AUTHOR, actually *all over* this noticer so there's no daylight, and you are secretly infecting it with your own little attitudes and wishfulness?

You teach yourself to be dispassionate, to trust the story. Meanwhile, you read the best writers who ever lived in order to study how they managed what they've managed, and realize great writers too make mistakes, which has always heartened me.

You study the mechanics of narrative time, seeing how the narrative actually does want everything to work right, for it to be its own all-inclusive domino race, that it's a closed system where everything results in something meaningful, that when the tree falls in the forest it's the novelist who's there to hear it.

⇒

THE BOOK IS being written. It will seem like it's being written in order to become its own study of the way a book must be written. It becomes a proof of the elements, After and Before, Beginning, Middle, and End, cause and effect. It becomes big enough to be round. It has its own natural laws, including gravity. It closes itself off and will no longer take in the one more thing you think you might like to add.

In its own closed universe, the novel—and this will eventually come to feel like a lowercase god who is simply bigger than you are and better than you will ever be—understands how every element is very intricately related to every other thing in the novelistic realm.

And this brings us comfort and solace as novelists, that a tiny flick of our fingernail can activate this entire beautiful network of action and interaction, that it *works*.

And we witness, with wonder, the logical apparatus whereby a story's forward motion keeps itself in motion all along the highways and byways over which it must travel to find its destination.

In these moments of amazement, we are given back everything we've put into this work, feeling that we've made something that brings the world amusement, surprise, and, yes, joy.

⇒

YOU GET LOST from your characters, you check back in. Narrative continuity demands that time continues even when there's no one noticing, that it's time that keeps everything rolling, that it all rolls on, that it was rolling before we came and will continue after we're gone:

> Which is exactly what Bob is thinking now that it's 3 AM and they're on Route 80 in a rest stop outside Iowa City, as this is how far they've come and where we will now go ahead to leave them.

Gigi's asleep in the top bunk, and Wesley Earl, who goes only by Bob, because his brothers teased him that Wesley Earl made him sound sissified, is on the bottom bunk that you get at by pulling it out from bulwark after folding the table in two parts up against the wall.

She helped you clean up the supper dishes. And you're flat-out confused by this girl, your kids are grown and gone, and maybe you're becoming a reckless person, now that your wife is gone and you've splurged on this top-of-the-line sleeper cab, which cost you nearly $60,000, and you're such a completely sentimental man you're already thinking that this child needs protection and tending, that all she probably lacks is a good college education and you have money in the bank.

Because you are a sweet, almost maternal man, almost preternaturally nice, which your wife, who was a hard case, called your *gullibility*. She called this trait by its name, as if it were the third person who lived with them. She'd pretend to hear it knocking on the door, when you'd be busy telling her some wild tale about someone you'd met on the road. Or she would, without interrupting, go pick up the phone as if it had been ringing and hand it to you saying, "Here, Hon, it's your gullibility."

Were she here, she'd say: You always were picking up strays, and with me not even one year dead, in a single day you've found yourself not one but two.

≥

YOU WILL DO a time check outside Iowa City for continuity, a time check for believability. You need to investigate a few things to notch this up into the realm of The Real, to understand where the long-haul trucker will park his rig halfway across Iowa, and investigate the rules regarding weigh-ins, because all of this is computerized these days, and a trucker is not allowed to drive more than ten hours a day, or whatever the limit really is. You need to understand that there are laws governing this, that Bob McGaw was once shut down and told to rest by the Interstate Commerce Commission agent, forced to hold up in Hellbox, Nevada, and asked to stay off the road for three days.

Bob McGaw doesn't drink, he doesn't smoke, he doesn't whore around, and he doesn't approve of gambling—which, he believes, takes money from the people who can afford it least. He gambled once, didn't like it, said it felt like he'd taken a pile of money out and had watched himself setting it on fire on the street.

The girl smokes, of course. They will have complicated arguments about this in the future of this story, the part that isn't yet written. He will tell her that smoking will stunt her growth, that she's too little to begin with, and while she *says* she is seventeen years old, she looks more like thirteen, fourteen at the most.

He'll say this as his heart is sinking. He has no reason to believe her when she tells him her age, as she is a through-and-through liar.

It was when they were talking about her size that he first heard her and knew he could read her mind. She said nothing aloud at all.

But she was looking him up and down, her pieced eyebrow arched, and why do these kids want to plug all this metal and crap into the skin of their faces? She has that barbell thing through her eyebrow and a sparkling jewel at the side of one nostril, but it's the bitten-away fingernails with black stuff on them that *really* bothers him. She doesn't look entirely clean, they'd have to have a talk on that, she also looks smug, also derisive, as she was dying to say what she didn't say, which was: *Stunt's a person's growth, does it? Huh? Well then maybe you should take it up.*

⮐

AND THE TWO are suddenly an Odd Couple, asymmetrical twins who act as foils for one another, who will tangle and fight and love one another fervently, and we know it's all right to ride along with them because the tone says this is a love story but one that operates in the grander, more novelistic way that feels larger than what is purely romantic.

How do we know all this is happening? They've been acquainted for no time at all and can already read each other's minds.

⇒

TIME CHECK. WEIGH IN. Getting your story grounded in its own physical reality, you look up "Peterbilt" on the Web and walk around in one, via video, in its most high-end cab, instantly realizing that you were born to be an interstate truck driver, how could you have lived as long as you have by now and missed this?

She's asleep in the top bunk, he's imagining the unimaginability of the future that contains a person like Gigi, or whatever her real name is, and she isn't seventeen, he's become absolutely convinced of this.

You check for time, for date, for global positioning, you check for your narrator's impartial state of mind. You check to vet the language of the storyteller, to make sure that you—The Author—hasn't infected it (see *authorial intrusion*).

You import language that you didn't know you knew; it was only three days ago that you knew none of these trucker words and now here look at you.

You roll the window down, you allow the language of the fictional world to come in through the open windows of the cab. All you must do is listen.

Here he comes back from the showers at the transit center. She has the dog in bed with her. He's shaved, cleaned, as new to the world as the grass-scented wind blowing off what used to be the prairie, and we suddenly have all kinds of hope for them because he is bringing the morning with him.

⇒

AND TO PROTECT the hope you have for your novel, please remember that no one, even yourself, should look at this initial draft critically. We do ourselves an enormous favor when we can turn off those critical voices and grant ourselves the freedom to get a preliminary draft down on paper. You want to quiet the voices that interfere with your being able to hear what the book itself is telling you.

And this is why—at this earliest of stages—I strongly suggest that you do whatever you can to protect the still-incipient and fragile nature of this plot-slash-little-story-like thing of yours that isn't quite a novel. You are only beginning to be able to hear as it is struggling to tell itself to you.

You do this by not allowing random people to read it yet. And who is a random person at this earliest of stages? Just about everyone you ever knew.

You don't show people your early writing because you don't really want to know what they think of it, of you. You don't reread your own work because you don't want to invite your own criticism in. Our own critical voices are always all over these things, sidewalk supervisors ignorantly asking if we don't really want a window over there.

We have spent our entire lives so far developing these amazing critical skills that allow us to discern good writing from bad. We've spent so much more time being critical than we have actually writing that the left-brained critic is always able to defeat the incipient novelist. Putting them in the ring together is like matching a pit bull against Bob's Chihuahua. No fair.

You guard this protoplotted, barely house-trained, only semireasonable, bug-eyed, eager, wiggling little thing of yours because it seems like it may want to grow up to become your novel.

THE MOST IMPORTANT lesson in writing a book-length book is that we cannot become dismayed or defeated by the overwhelming nature of length and breadth and weight of the narrative materials. We drive the fourteen to eighteen wheelers, hauling thirteen tons of household furnishings, boxes and boxes of what is either gold or trash, which—by the way—weighs the same at the truck scales. That most of the cargo is books matters only to those of us—you and me, the novelists—who read them and write them.

The trick is not to be buried by all the material our narrative is forced to slosh and carry back and forth across this grand land of ours. We simply learn to trust and to take it on faith that plot and story will work together to *sort it all out*, if not now then eventually.

As they do, your novel's sense of its own reality will accrete. It will soon begin to drive on because it's become used to the process and in so doing picks up narrative momentum. This feels like self-confidence, feels like you're riding high in this huge very powerful truck cab that lets you look down on lesser mortals.

The writing has its own halo effect, the doing of it produces the feeling that you can actually do it.

The proof?

Here you are doing it.

PART TWO

What follows are evolving definitions of the
tools and concepts I've found useful and necessary
in thinking about the longer narrative.

The ABCs of Narrative Structure

A

ABCs: The basics of good storytelling are easy, and they are these: *Action, background, development, Crisis,* and *Ending.* We use the shorthand AbdCE and call this a story's *line of action* or the *arc of the narrative.*

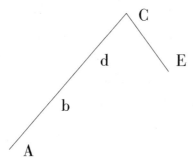

We all intuitively know this narrative shape; we're well acquainted with the rhythms of effective storytelling from the experience of telling stories and having them told to us. We know how a good story will naturally build toward *revelation*, understanding that *surprise* is a crucial element in keeping us interested. A story must at first hide its revelations from us so that we can feel as if we, too, are participants in the solving of its mysteries.

Action is so important to a story that we set it apart with a capital letter, as we do with both *Crisis* and *Ending*. Less crucial are *background* and *development* (of *plot* or *theme* or *character*). Background and development, if left alone, tend to take care of themselves.

The C marks the hinge. This is the story's highest point, where *the reason* we're being told this story (or this segment of the story) suddenly becomes apparent. C also stands for *clarity*, also *conflict, crisis, complication, change*.

The longer narrative moves in an *anticipatory direction*, always powered upward by the feeling of *expectation*.

The narrative uses a story's energy to catapult it from stasis into movement that works *because of* conflict. A scene works through conflict toward its resolution and then on toward the moment of conflict or complication.

At the highest C—the story's climax—is found the narrative hinge where both speed and directionality change. At the apex we glimpse the larger, more magisterial view of the whole. Suddenly the narrative elements can be seen in their totality, from *Beginning* to *End*. Here we finally comprehend not only where the Beginning starts but also why it must start exactly there. We see the parts arranging their own integration as they stand in both causal and sequential relationship, which make sense of the *plotline* and the *storyline*.

Abstracted isosceles (see also *sprung triangle*): The ABCs diagram describes the shape made by opening a triangle that has roughly two equal sides and one that is fundamentally shorter. By springing the narrative triangle open at its hinges, a tension is introduced that enlivens its events and incidents.

The tension decrees that each element matters to the story and is part of the plot's various dilemmas. Resolving these will result in the sprung triangle being unsprung, that is, the Ending and the Beginning will snap back into a solid, stable figure.

The sprung shape of the narrative means it triangulates upward, moving always in the hidden direction of its inevitable return to its unsprung form.

Action: The narrative is born of action. Action is not made of our thoughts, nor does it easily arise from memory alone. Action instead comprises meaningful events and incidents that happen along the line of the story, actions that move according to the rules of plot.

Events become meaningful to the degree that they move the action along the arc of the narrative in an anticipatory direction.

Action moves by way of its ARC: *action, reaction, change.* Change is built into any meaningful action. A meaningful action has a cause-and-effect relationship to other events and incidents along the plotline. It takes place before the witness of our senses, so we gain *haptic knowledge* of this event. This means it is seen, heard, touched, tasted, smelled, felt as a physical and psychological experience.

Writing *in* action has a different character and tension from writing that *describes* an action, at some remove from the storyline. These descriptions—summary of scene—belong to the plotline, where we speed through events that contain no meaningful action. We do this to elaborate upon a character's background or to sum up a scene that has happened at another time and place.

Writing *in* action imparts a sense of risk: It is happening before our eyes and ears, so we cannot yet know how it is going to turn out. We don't know the narrative consequences of this action and cannot predict the future. Action can be said, therefore, to contain a legitimate narrative future in the way summary of scene contains the narrative past.

A story goes dead without *risk*.

Affective states: We read not only with our intellectual, reasoning minds but with our emotions. These feeling states are regulated by particular areas of the brain to render meaning more immediately than does "thought," through what we might call gut reaction. This happens subliminally through bodily cues that direct our attention to certain elements of the story, allowing us to know things—such as a sense of creepiness or a distrust of a character—before we have accumulated evidence to prove his untrustworthiness. Through the activity of these affective areas of the brain, we will get a character's behavior before we can intellectually understand their motivations.

It is through the affective realm of thinking that we assess the narrative environment as being dangerous or safe. This happens *exactly* as we figure these things out in real life.

The writer and the reader are both entirely dependent on extremely subtle affective clues that hover around the words a writer uses. These clues are also offered by what is *not* done, *not* said—for instance, the utter lack of affection demonstrated between the married couples in the chilly rooms of the affluent 1960s, as seen in the masterly TV series *Mad Men*.

The narrative, then, is a whole-brain activity that asks for a balance between what the writing makes us *think*—the cognitive functions of our minds—and what the writing makes us *feel*, as bodily knowledge and sensation.

After and Before: These linked principles of narrative structure help define the all-important relationships of cause and effect. Action causes a reaction or effect and therefore contains within it the reaction that results in change.

After and Before work with sequencing and with cause and effect to both show and hide relationships of characters and events along a novel's plotline. Every event and incident is related to every other along the line of the story, though the meaning of these relationships is kept hidden until we reach the novel's climax and ensuing resolution.

The narrative likes to come upon a cause and wait for its effect, which imbues the tension of the link in the storyline. We anticipate the effect to show up as *consequence*. A narrative's action is made up of the story's Now, as seen *in scene*, together with this scene's After, which is the consequence of its actions, determined largely by what has come Before.

Ambient time: This is the name for that sense of time that seems both general and yet standing slightly to the side of the arc of the narrative. I think of it as *Light in August* time in that it carries a grand sense of spaciousness.

Ambient time feels dreamy and imparts the feeling of comfort to the narrative, saying it's a safe place to enter. We use it to move into a different temporal zone of the narrative or as an active lull, for its feeling of safety and timelessness.

Ambient time will also echo and resonate with its ability to foreshadow the safe harbor in which the longer narrative will eventually come to rest at the novel's Ending. Ambient time is written, therefore, to mimic our sense of ordinary time, in its day-to-day, its always-ness, the kind of time that lacks those active incidents and events to which the story must now, if reluctantly, return.

Ambient time is useful for pacing and to precede the first piece of action set in a new time and place. It thereby allows the reader to settle into a change in the story's new situation before being slammed with the narrative's need to *move on!* as it always must, in its relentless quest for meaning.

Ambient time feels introductory, also accumulative, as if it subtly anticipates highly dramatic episodes. It can also be used to signal a shift from point of view, marking a place where a new storyline begins, and—as such—contains the resting place found in the balance of a story's resolution.

We can use this quality of time to build what we call the *narrative pause*. From this pause, we will enter a new part, section, or chapter from on high, getting a point of view that can feel godlike or objective.

"It was the best of times, it was the worst of times," from Charles Dickens's *A Tale of Two Cities*, is an example of a book's starting in the overarching omniscience of ambient time. It then goes on a few paragraphs later to settle down in the specificity of the novel's Now, which is Paris and London in 1775.

Anecdote: This is a story in perhaps its most encapsulated and incidental form. It will seem tossed off, as if the narrator is creating it spontaneously.

The writer may have an anecdotal style (as I do), which allows her to confide what seems to be an aside. This must, however, turn out to be an intrinsic part of the plot, subplot, or corollary theme. Otherwise this anecdote, amusing as it may at first seem, will have to go. Here's an anecdote I just rescued from the location in which it had been misplaced, under the entry **etymological fallacy:** The American language works in the direction of its own ability to be plainspoken. I once fired a literary agent because he used the word *postprandial*. "Shall we meet before lunch?" he asked me, "or should this happen postprandially?"

I think he thought this usage was amusing. It made me incalculably furious. *And this guy is supposed to be a* literary *agent?* I thought. *What an asshole. Has he even read my work?*

When I fired him I said, "Please believe me, this has nothing to do with our professional relationship. My decision is entirely personal."

Angles: Your episodes are built on the tipped model of the A-C-E triangle (see **ABCs**). This moves the action along the narrative arc, away from stasis and at a particular angle, either steep or gradual, as set by the kind of story your book seems to want to be. A thriller begins in the acute angle that marks its slam-bang intensity. This will happen immediately, as it sets out hugely dramatic actions: a murder, a bank heist, a kidnapping. A novel of self-discovery will climb according to a narrative angle that is gentler, quieter, more oblique. This book, too, might feature the death of a character as an event, but it will climb toward this action, coming upon it more gradually.

Antecedent action: The antecedent action is the logical narrative trigger that launches a *flashback*. The two episodes sit side by side, flopped in chronology, the one coming first on the storyline, the other coming first on the plotline. They sit next to each other so we can see the mind of the book creating this *direct causal relationship*. The way the two episodes work can be solved only backward, in what the logic of plotting calls the inevitability of retrospect.

In *Slumdog Millionaire*, for instance, the boy on the quiz show is asked a question that then prompts, or causes, the story's ensuing episodes to spin out in flashback. This causal relationship is best expressed as *because*: Because I experienced the following actions—those actions shown within the unspooling time of the series of episodes in this flashback—I came to know the answer to the question being asked of me in the story's present time. The question being posed is the *prompt*.

The antecedent action, as well as the *flash-forward* or flashback that is bonded to it, presumes a united and linked psychological mechanism that mimics the way every individual actually does think. One thought will prompt another according to this individual's logic. The narrative chooses these logical links, though this logic is sometimes hidden in an apparent brush with randomness. Or it is twisted into a form of logic (such as psychosis) that feels illogical and is difficult to follow, yet follows its own pattern of regular irregularity.

The logic of story's thought cannot be predictive, because a story deals only with the immediate and cannot know its own future.

The mind of the book, however, which is truly omniscient, can know the ending and so awards plot the ability to flash-forward to events that have not yet happened.

Anterior narrative: This contains everything that lies before and has led up to the present moment of the episode. Any event lying off the storyline may seem random but will eventually prove itself to be part of the anterior narrative. (If it hopes to remain in this particular story.) An aside or a digression must always be only a tributary to the forward rush and current of the anterior narrative, by leading back toward the line of action.

Anticipatory direction: A story asks always to enact itself by embarking on its own journey. It is only through the writing of its episodes that a story is able to show whatever incidents and events this narrative contains.

A novel's mood is anticipatory and angles upward to be suspenseful. Suspense contributes to the feeling that this is real, because in real life we can never predict what will occur from day to day in any given future's infinite possibilities. Therefore, suspense is a vital element in each ticking moment of reality.

Apex: This is the place along the arc of the narrative where the story turns, all vectors change direction, and all matters raised in its long beginning start to be resolved.

A vector is a fatter or thinner, longer or shorter arrow of directionality and force. It indicates the power of this character or event or narrative situation to alter the course of the story. After the apex, these will move as quickly as they can to the story's Ending.

This occurs as the story and all its dynamic elements alter directions and begin to race toward what will *feel* like the novel's ending. The pace of the story quickens, as if the ending itself were being raised by its own system of winches, gears, and pulleys, the ground coming up to meet the events that are diving toward it.

The apex is marked on the ABCs plotting diagram at the highest C, which stands for the *crisis*, toward which our plot, story, and characters are all drawn. After the apex is reached, the gravitational force shifts to the Ending, which then takes over this same insistence and pull.

Aptonym: This fictional device allows a writer to give a character a name that exactly fits and reinforces his job or social status:

Father Church, the Episcopal priest; Mr. Garland, the florist; Farmer Cornsilk. Often used for comic effect, an aptonym is usually assigned to a flat character; it will be impossible for the rounder, more fully developed character to change if given one. This is one more reason we need to weigh carefully what we call every one of our characters.

ARC (action-reaction-change): Action, reaction, change—as *witnessed* by the narrator and the reader together—are the only dynamic sources of narrative energy. They allow the story's events to propel it in the onward-and-upward direction of an almost infinite sense of narrative possibility.

Arc of the narrative: Your episodes will be arranged in the story along the rising *arc of the narrative*, which describes the transition from thesis to antithesis to synthesis. The narrative works always in an anticipatory direction that asks: *And then?*

Aristotle: He calls the movement of the AbdCE a story's *unraveling*. A novel is built with starts and stops, like a narrative game of Chutes and Ladders. It is moving always in the direction of its own completion, a downhill run where tempo changes as a story cascades into its earthbound resolution. It finds itself again at rest.

Arrows of time: In real life, the drag of time runs only one way, from birth toward death. In the longer narrative, time is carefully plotted and allowed and encouraged to play tricks. These are called various things, including *asides, flash-forwards, digressions, flashbacks, impacted memories, embedded memories, memory triggers, free associations*. These narrative devices work to give a novel a realistic and effective texture and as a relief from the relentlessness with which it works in the day-to-day.

The arrows of time in your story will belong to the human realm, *always* to someone or something. This could be a character, the narrator, or even a place; through it we feel human and mortal and understand our own complex relationships with our mortality. The arrows of time within the duration of a single episode always run in the customary direction in which time is marked off by the scene's *internal duration*. The *external duration* of the story, however, allows for all kinds of manipulations of time, whereby individual episodes are placed here or there along the line of action, always with a mind toward their chronological and causal relationships.

Indeed, one of the great subjects of contemporary literature is the manner in which our perception of narrative time can be altered. Single episodes can be moved here or there, or written in warped time to seem dreamlike, or experienced in the hyper-realism of nightmare.

The following books successfully manipulate the tissue of the time within the narrative so Time itself becomes a character and is an important element in plotting: Charles Baxter's *First Light*, Jim Crace's *Being Dead*, and Shirley Hazzard's *The Transit of Venus*. Time is also an element in the plotting of the following movies, in which the pieces of the clockwork are taken apart and rearranged in a manner that plays with temporal reality: *Pulp Fiction*, *Total Recall*, *Memento*, *Dead Again*, *Babel*, *21 Grams*, and *Inside Man*.

Associative logic: This principle of narrative derives from mathematics and depth psychology. Each notes the way the human mind thinks.

Association says that two similar objects or occurrences go together regardless of the order in which they are presented, that the mind will sort these and provide the link that splices them logically together. This relieves the writer of the need to *point out* these links, as the reader already gets it either consciously or subliminally.

The mechanics of associative logic are as simple as this: Two characters arrive at a scene simultaneously. We will associate the two as being in relationship with one another, though their arrival may turn out to be coincidental.

"Involuntary memory," which works along the lines of the same associative pathways, is a term coined by Marcel Proust, who used the "episode of the madeleine" to name the sensation of being swamped by an overwhelming sense of the very vivid past as he bit into a certain cookie.

Associative logic can be seen in the work of such narrative devices as *flashback* and *embedded memory*, which have their own entries.

Authorial intrusion: This is the writer's coming so close to the scene that his or her voice is heard on the page when we're expecting only those voices that actually belong there. The author simply doesn't get a voice on the page of his or her book: All language within a narrative belongs either to the story's characters or to its narrator or as an import from the language of the world.

Authorial intrusion—when done intentionally, for effect—is an old device that wants to feel new and clever but will often come off as clumsy and antique. It is the Victorians' "Dear Reader" revamped as metafiction, in which the Author pops up in costume, disguised as a character.

An Author becomes a character the moment he or she enters into the narrative space that the narrative scene creates—and this notion is so often left uncalculated by the fiction writer. My first encounter with Author as a somewhat menacing character riding along in the same railroad car as a character, thinking, *Okay, what am I going to do with you now?* felt inventive when I first read it. That was in John Fowles's *The French Lieutenant's Woman.* The year was 1969.

In order to add to the narrative, the device must be used in a sufficiently fresh way to get around the reader's resentment that the narrative dream has been interrupted. Most often, inexperienced writers intrude upon their narrative without understanding that they are doing it. Flagging lines of dialogue with not-very-helpful prompts is the most subtle sign of an intrusive author, the one who writes a perfectly good line of speech, then feels the need to tell the reader how these lines are being read, as in this hospital scene:

> "Would you like me to? Would you like to play a game of Scrabble, Mother?" Katrinka asked. She touched the shine on Winnie's worried forehead.
>
> "Oh, I suppose," Winnie admitted.
>
> "Is there anything else we can bring you? Do you want a hamburger from Bob's Big Boy, with two pieces

of real meat in it? Would you like me to bring you a bottle of scotch?"

"I do not drink," Winnie announced.

"Well, maybe you ought to start," Katrinka informed her.

This is from my first novel, *Failure to Zigzag*. My characters are *admitting* and *announcing* and *informing*, because the book's author was young and didn't yet trust that her reader would *get* the way a line of speech is said if she did her job and wrote it so that it read on the page the way it was supposed to.

In its unintentional form, authorial intrusion is simply evidence of our profound wishfulness that certain things be understood. If they are already happening in the scene, then this goes without saying. If they are not yet happening in the scene, the writer simply has another little bit of work ahead of her.

Another reason authorial intrusion so often backfires: Almost no one cares about how clever you and I think we are. Our stories don't usually care much about us, either: We are merely the vessels through which this version of this old and ancient story is being poured, *this time*.

Less about you, our stories seem to say to us, and more about how to get this novel to participate in the vast narrative timelessness.

Axis of asymmetry: This imaginary line runs through the arc of narrative. It marks where the story's balance shifts from the vector of its rising action into its *falling action*, or *denouement*. The axis of asymmetry decrees that the story is now tipped and is traveling toward its Ending.

B

Background: Background is past tense in relationship to what is currently happening along the Now of the scene. Because its events have already happened and this action is concluded, background is no longer open to change and is therefore no longer a dynamic element.

This is why, when you're importing great chunks of explanatory background, the experience feels deadening.

Writers who feel that they must tell us about background before a story is allowed to start delay the moment when these events begin to show or reveal themselves of their own accord. This isn't really the narrative's best use of background, which wants to be imported as something that might have life brought back to it.

It becomes dynamic because the "facts" have suddenly been allowed to change. A character will happen upon an element from his or her past and suddenly *see* this event or person or situation in a new way.

When apropriately used, background can set the trajectory of a character's vector as he or she enters the story. Any long-winded explanation of what the writer mistakenly considers "all that the reader needs to know" delays the moment of Now. It halts our ultimate entry into what the film director Bernardo Bertolucci called the cathedral of art. It is here that we feel involved with—and viscerally encapsulated within—the story's *action*.

Background must be slipped into a story almost invisibly, or it will lie on top and smother the action. Background need not stand in the foyer of your story and announce itself, which will stop the story as it pulls everyone's attention to this announcement. Background in a story should demonstrate itself only as it becomes absolutely necessary.

The principle of artistic unity decrees that a character is a sum of his or her every past experience, up to and including the moment in which he or she is permitted to act. This means that background is enacted in the character's behavior, in the manner in which he or she comes alive—to speak, move, think, and act.

Backstory: A backstory unfolds chronologically earlier (in terms of *actual time*, not mere page placement) than the larger narrative.

A backstory informs the behavior of the larger narrative's participants, but it lies off the narrative arc and will not be shown to us in direct episodes.

We can think of backstory as the history of our characters or of other elements that underlie the story's present situation. This history exists at the start of the narrative, what Henry James would call a particular story's or character's *donnée*.

Backstory is used to lend depth and a sense of verisimilitude to the main story, in that we understand everyone to have come from somewhere and to be headed somewhere else. The dramatic revelation of secrets from the backstory is a technique recognized since the time of Aristotle.

Backstories are usually revealed fully or partially, chronologically or otherwise as the main narrative naturally unfolds. Many writers first develop entire life histories for their characters, histories that will never be shown in their stories, so they can better understand their characters' actions. I don't. I trust my characters to show what they're going to reveal naturally. I assume that my characters have dark secrets because, honestly, don't we all?

Balance: It produces a pleasing, proportionate, or harmonious arrangement among the parts of any composition. A narrative always starts in imbalance and works in the direction of harmony by resolving each of its conflicts. It finally arrives at what will feel like the narrative home of its Ending.

Before and After: All episodes in the longer narrative sit in the temporal relationship to one another described by Before and After, except when we are weaving together two pieces of fictional time that occur simultaneously (when, for instance, the arrows of narrative time are following the actions of two characters who haven't yet interacted).

All actions earn their way into the story by proving themselves significant to the narrative's outcome (see **After and Before**).

Before versus Ago: The word *before* marks a specific time in direct relationship to the moment in which an episode occurs. "They started their vacation pile a few days before, which consisted, so far, of what they would need on their trip: sunscreen, passports, the brochure from their seaside villa." The word *ago* is better used in dialogue, when the character says, for instance, "I started adding stuff to that pile three days ago." We can then understand the precision with which time is being marked.

The appearance of either *before* or *ago* asks that the writer do a time check to establish the temporal situation of all narrative parties, including characters, noticer, and narrator.

Beginning: In Aristotle's view the Beginning is that element of plot that needs no other event to anticipate it. A story begins when the first significant action takes place. The action occurs in a certain specific time and place in which the scene shows characters engaged in meaningful conflict. This conflict will lead to the story's inevitable outcome.

The Beginning falls, as Aristotle tells us, *exactly* where the Ending starts, and in this quality they are forever and always linked.

Broken symmetries: Pattern and repetition come with the longer-narrative writer's tool kit, but we want to break these patterns. We want to move the plot from balance and make room for the unexpected. A broken symmetry does this by placing three characters, not two, in conflict. Or, say, by giving a character three choices: Do this, do that, or (the symmetry breaker) do nothing.

Broken symmetries feel *lifelike* to us because they mirror the splintered—or *fractal*—nature of reality, in which nothing breaks into two symmetrical parts.

C

The *C* Words: The narrative drives toward these fictive events, these spiritual motivators that cause the action to be perceived as meaningful. They include crisis, conflict, change, climax, consequence, conclusion, chance.

Cardinal numbers in sequencing: These are called the "counting numbers," our good old 1, 2, 3. These are profoundly important to us, in that they reference a story's sense of its own interior chronology.

Time is God's way of arranging for events to occur in an orderly fashion, according to the story's 1, 2, 3.

Plot, however, will come along to mess with this basic plan, which is *chronology*, by saying, *That's boring; we probably are going to need to come upon these events in a somewhat different order.* Plot assigns their *ordinal numeration*, that is, the showing forth or revelation: *first, second, third.*

If I knew anything about playing even the simplest musical instrument, I could here employ an apt metaphor, telling you how the story is playing the order with the piano keys with the right hand while plot is way down the keyboard pounding out the ordinal, but it doesn't exactly work like that. A novel is built of both kinds of order playing out against each other and with each other. They do this in a kind of respectful tension that dances around and through and up and down the temporal line of its own events. This is accomplished by an intricate play on time that is established by the narrative's very organized sense of temporal logic, in its After and Before, Cause and Effect. A story's working out its own rather plain chronology—while staying open to plot's need for dramatic sequencing—is often wonderful to behold.

Cause and Effect: The causal nature of every coherent story asks that each event and incident have significance to the larger narrative whole. A story, unlike life, is exacting in its use of causal logic. Our minds are always engaged by our need to solve for cause, that the car was going too fast to round the sharp bend in the road without mishap. One reason a story gains momentum is by mounting ongoing proofs against these subliminal tests of narrative logic. A story, in fact, feels more and more beautifully made to the degree to which its events feels "true" in matters of cause and effect.

Every action must ultimately demonstrate its worth and meaning to the story's sum. Each incident and event must earn its place by showing that it moves the story along the narrative arc toward the story's Ending, which sits (according to narrative logic) in front of the discovery of its Beginning.

A story does this by means of its ability to sort and match significant actions, linkages provided by cause and effect. Each action is eventually shown to have been caused by another significant action, which will in turn cause other significant events.

Events and incidents linked by the logic of cause and effect should be separated by other, unlinked episodes, to create suspense. Cause and effect demand this resonating tension in each other, as if they are speaking to each other along the line of the story. This energy holds the longer narrative together, united and taut.

Episodes play out in order to demonstrate that their actions are indeed significant. They prove this by delivering the story, via cause and effect, from one side of a conflict or crisis to the other side. This change in narrative direction illustrates where the story needs to go to find its next significant complication.

Significance is established by working within the timeline of all cause-and-effect relationships. An effect always lies *chronologically* after its cause. Plot, however, may ask that a story first show the effect, then work backward down the storyline to discover how the story is linked by cause.

Episodes are causally magnetized to one another through our basic need for logic and coherence in a narrative, which operates much more powerfully in art than it does in real life.

In real life we assume that random events will not necessarily come forth to help us make coherent narrative sense of things. In real life, particularly tragic events, such as needless loss of life, often seem "senseless" or "without logical meaning."

The closed system of the narrative, however, asks that all events at least subliminally speak across time to establish their relationship. They forge meaning out of chaos, so that an effect will always have a cause. Cause and effect may be separated from each other by hundreds of pages, many decades, or entire continents of narrative geography. Yet they can still speak to each other's significance, establishing a sense of narrative unity.

Certainty: We read—we also write—because we seek shelter from real life's uncertainty, says memoirist Brenda Miller in *Season of the Body*: "While I read I believed, without knowing it, in the certitude of the narrative: that all beginnings inevitably lead to some kind of conclusion. I believed a story began at some predetermined point in time and moved steadily forward toward its inborn resolution. These two parts did not change—the beginning remained the beginning, the conclusion remained the end—no matter how often I read the stories, or how long I stayed away. I found a stunning comfort in this symmetry, this permanence."

Chance: A narrative is a closed system in which there is no room for chance. Yet the narrative tricks us into believing that chance is as much in play as it is in our real lives, that every narrative moment has the ability to surprise us with its seeming quality of sheer randomness. A novel uses a web carefully woven of narrative coincidence, using events and incidents that must occur, according to the Gods of Plot, but still have the casual texture of everyday accident. Everything must, in fact, feel accidental, spontaneous, as if it is happening because of the element of luck.

In our stories people will *get lucky* with more dependable regularity than they do in real life; their lives will feel charmed. They will seem to be blessed, watched over by provenance. You and I probably experience this feeling of exhilarated meaning only at births and weddings and funerals, where a curtain is drawn back and our lives suddenly seem *to make narrative sense.*

So we *enjoy* watching the careful way a narrative arranges for our characters to get lucky in a longer narrative. Our Gigi, from Part One, hops in the cab of a truck driver who is a kind man, and lonely; he isn't an axe murderer or a child abuser. Our characters getting lucky makes us feel like someone or something—the Gods of Plot, the mind of the book—*is* in control. Maybe these same gods are at work in our own lives, that everything *is* somehow happening for a reason. But our rational minds will always argue, *Sorry, honey, but it's randomness all the way backward, forward, up one side and down the other.*

But chance, when at work in a story, makes us forget that the Gods of Plot are powerless to rig a game show. In the movie *Slumdog Millionaire* it was theoretically possible that the main character might not have guessed the name of the third musketeer. And yet he did, because he actually had to, as decreed by the Gods of Plot, in that the answer (which we find written in the credits) is "D: It is written."

Change: This may be the most important element that plot delivers to the longer narrative's story. Change is the test of every action or event—and also of every character who is perceived to be alive. Each element can be asked, in order to assess its narrative usefulness, what potential for *change* does this offer?

Chapters: The chapter is a structural unit that derives from ancient scripture and is simply less useful for the writer of the longer narrative than are these more descriptive terms: *scene* and *episode.* A chapter is a vessel that may hold one scene or several scenes. It may be organized according to theme or matters of logic or sequence or causation. It may be used to shift time or point of view.

A chapter may be almost any size, from single scene to *very* long. It may be an amalgamation of episodes, which are set into context using various kinds of narrative time. A chapter, therefore, isn't conceptually *anything* until plot decides on its use. This happens *later*, when the chapter is assigned its ordinal number— whether it comes first, second, third in the book.

The numbers are assigned *later*, after plot has had a chance to organize episodes so that they resonate.

Characters: Our characters have the job of carrying the action of the story from one complication to the next inevitable complication, working always in the direction of change. Characters may be drawn directly from life, yet they are not exactly people. This is why, for example, real people so often object to their portrayals in our narratives even though every word they utter in our version of reality is verifiably what they have truly uttered in real life.

Real people lie outside the writer's control, whereas *characters* are our creations and act within our dominion.

Characters are less complex than actual people. Characters are always artistically simplified for the streamlined narrative purpose of the job they need to do. A character is a *porter of action*. He or she should be felt to be *alive* or *real* (or *round* in E. M. Forster's terminology), if she or he can be seen to be engaged by narrative time and perceived by us as mortal. This means the character is susceptible to *change*, birth, growth, sickness, evolution, transformation.

Round characters, as Forster says, have the incalculability of life about them, so their actions cannot be predicted. Round characters will also seem to move in the direction of *choice*. Because of this, they seem to exhibit the property of free will. Flat characters—which may still be elaborately drawn—must enter and exit a story essentially unchanged. Flat characters also seem to embody *types* of humans rather than *actual, specific* humans. Flat characters often suffer under the weight of single, all-defining traits: their race or ethnicity; their age; their caste, class, or regional situation; their gender; their "otherness."

Caste, class, ethnicity, age, and gender inform our round characters as well. But a round character exists within the narrative situation that has arrived to particularize him or her, to call this character out from the multitude and create this singular individual.

The round character cannot be said to actually exist without the narrative's action—it is up to the story to create the scenes that enliven our living characters.

They are then twisted into the plot in all the various ways that feel like real life, which is fraught with conflict and complication. We can then see the tension of the characters' inner selves as they interact with the external world. This interaction defines their setting in narrative time and place, their story's situation.

They interact with plot by being presented with a *dilemma* that must worsen into *crisis*, demanding that your characters take *action* to resolve this crisis. They do this by moving on, always in the direction of *change*.

Characters in action: It is the story that moves our characters; our characters do not move the story. Action infuses the story with the sense that time is alive and passing, that the characters' actions move them from a position of rest and calm in the direction of the next complication or conflict.

Change is achieved as characters in action move always in the direction of conflict, through conflict, and on toward the next conflict. The energy from these forces' opposition moves the story in its upward direction along the narrative arc, always toward anticipation. They achieve this sense of ascendancy by being pulled along from meaningful incident to event by the twisted rope of the narrative complication.

The character in action will move always through triangulated points of conflict, as depicted in a meaningful scene or episode. A scene or episode becomes meaningful because its outcome contributes to the plot—that is, it lies along the line of action.

Cliché: An expression can be so worthy that it's sweet, hot, crazy, mad, so sick that it rocks, even kills! Until—no more than a *nanosecond* later!—it begins to curdle, molder, rot in overuse. Clichés are time-stamped, seeming to have the freshness baked in for just a little minute longer, right up until the point of not-so-much.

Worn out, they become prop words and dummy phrases, subbing for the language that wants to say something new, in that it is active or expressive.

To tell you the truth, we all speak in clichés. Why? We're human, we're in a rush, we live 24/7 in the meat world, and we can't help ourselves. And do our characters speak in clichés? You betcha, Red Rider, some of 'em speak in nothing but clichés, and some are so allergic to cliché they're rendered speechless. Clichés can be *used*, in other words, to define a character's habits of speech, such as his or her need to pun or tell jokes. They are so beautifully stamped that they create an eerily accurate sense of the temporal world, which is what it is: awesome.

A writer, crafting a first or second or third or fifteenth draft, needn't fuss about his or her own use of these chunks of edging-toward-antiquated language: No worries, s'all good, whatev . . . There's plenty of time later on to figure out whether these artifacts of common speech are working for or against you.

Climax: Beyond the hinge at the highest C, no new characters may be introduced, no new problems or complications may arise. The story has turned and now cascades toward resolution.

This movement is called the *denouement*, or *falling action*. The denouement follows the hinge, where the story changes in both speed and directionality. At the highest C a narrative settles into its own sense of inevitability.

Clockwork: Episodic time comprises such logical links as After and Before, Effect and its Cause, all working silently together in clockwork so fine and intricate that we barely notice it. Logic is *always at work*. Its job is to solve the narrative and is always figuring out how every element relates to every other element. Every incident, event, action, character, theme, and setting will finally be linked to all other aspects by the elegance of this spare and exacting narrative logic. The logic works because of and in accordance with the story's temporal coherence. Episodes will feel bonded to one another across great fields of geographic space and time, solving one another as the story works toward its own sum.

The longer narrative demands that each of its incidents and events stand in relationship to all other incidents and events, that it be reduced to its simplest form: its solution.

After and Before instruct us where our episodes lie in their most plain chronology, where they are written to establish a story's *external duration*. After and Before want to be separated along the arc of the narrative, spaced so that the distance is allowed to energize all narrative events that stand between them. We therefore feel the pulse of their sprung relationship.

You use this same device of narrative separation to pace the story's events. You work always to help the longer narrative in its wish to balance the arc—through not only action-reaction-change but *revelation* and *concealment*.

Closure: The abstracted *isosceles triangle* (see entry) must *close* upon itself to imply the feeling of psychological completion. This is crucial to the longer narrative. It's where its Ending and its Beginning meet and, therefore, define one another as such.

Closure is a borrowing from architectural discussion, and has also been imported into the studies of grief and loss. Does closure of old wounds and grievances actually exist? To what degree can anyone free himself or herself from the tragedies of history? Because we cannot really know the answer to this, great novelists will never stop writing great books.

Clues: Every person, place, and thing called out by your narrator's noticing becomes a clue in the mystery of your narrative. Each clue adds to the sum of the story and helps solve its overarching questions: What is happening? When and where is this taking place? Who is noticing these actions? How is the reality of the scene being conveyed?

Coincidence: The making of plot and subplot in the longer narrative is nothing more than the artful hiding of manipulated coincidence, whereby characters seem to meet by chance when they actually have no alternative.

A plot is woven of coincidence, which we can best understand by breaking the word apart—into *co* and *incidents*—and calling our story's occurrences its co-incidents, two incidents that met along the *line of action*, letting the story's characters interact significantly.

The sense of co-incidents makes the longer narrative appear to be an organized and knowable reality governed by one unified psychology—one that belongs to the narrator. The element of coincidence contributes to the sense that the story achieves the texture of reality, by casting its web out and around the chance occurrence.

Comedy: The Greeks considered this a less worthy form, less noble, than tragedy, which must advance its cause in a stately manner by its characteristic slow degrees.

Comedy's pace is quicker, operating out of the surprises of the moment. It is therefore more transient—what seems funny one moment may, in the next moment, not be funny in the least. Comedy works in context, as we all know, and with matters of likeness, often by imitating the more humble and base aspects of the human psyche.

Homer's *Iliad* and *Odyssey* are said to be the first epics to have encompassed both the comedic and tragic. Shakespeare, meanwhile, often punctuates his greatest tragedies with comedic asides. These serve as twins of the main strand of the narrative with low characters, who mirror and play off the tragic, or high characters, who stand at the heart of the drama. His comedies will end in balances, in matches, in what's been lost being found, the happy ending; while his tragedies end in loss that teaches us life's grim reality.

Many of us who work in a comedic vein understand how hard it is to be funny. Shakespeare's funny because he is a genius: Almost every genius is secretly funny, including the darkest writers you can bring to mind.

Command clause: We add these interjections parenthetically— *Will you look at that?*—to another phrase. This kind of verbal gesture captures the feel of spoken language: We think, notice, and therefore speak in a disjointed and interruptive manner.

Concealment: Elements in plot want to be concealed, unveiled only by *slow degrees*. We want to come upon new elements of the story with a sense of recognition. We want our senses to confirm that *this*, *too*, is meaningful and that we've been led to this meaning by the mechanisms of plot. Without being startled or bored, we should feel *That's right!* about whatever happens next.

Conclusion: A story's Ending and its Beginning are wed in metaphysical ways that we continue to harp on here. This is one good reason for the writer of the longer narrative to write a draft through to its narrative conclusion, whereby you throw a net over the last of its events and can feel its scope and duration.

Conflict: The movement in any story or episode of a story works in the direction of conflict, moving toward resolution of this conflict, then onward to meet plot's next conflict. Narrative energy gives the story its sense of possibility, that a future is being discovered by the plot's mechanics. These mechanics are moving the events upward toward their own ascendancy.

The traditional conflicts are conflict with oneself, conflict with God, conflict with nature, conflict with society, and conflict with particular others. These others may also seem to embody elements of God or nature or society.

Faulkner has said that all the best fiction comes "from the heart in conflict with itself." A character must act to discern the nature of the world. His or her behavior establishes the morality of the narrator's worldview. A character is pressed toward the solution of his or her interior conflict, which might be stated: How shall I act in *this* situation?

The modern character must experience interior conflict, or there is no opportunity in your novel for spiritual growth or doubt or moral choice. The opportunities for spiritual growth and doubt and moral choice are what define a character as round and his or her situation as modern.

Connotation: This is a more personal or emotional association, indirect and aroused by language, as opposed to the more "objective," dictionary-based denotation.

The novelist uses both the connotation and the denotation of words and phrases to deepen the story. Connotation and denotation will change according to the point of view of the speaker of this language. The language either (1) belongs to the narrator, (2) belongs to a character, or (3) exists within the story as language of the outside world. We might call this third option the *language of situation.*

Consequence: An action along the line of the story is united to other events in the causal manner that says an act has consequence. This means that every action, speech, event, person, place, or thing that lies along the narrative arc will eventually be shown to be in active relationship, in time and setting, to every other action, speech, event, person, place, or thing.

A plot is woven of events and incidents lying in the grid of their temporal and causal relationships. It becomes the web strung so that the spider senses the motion of interactions along every one of its interrelated threads.

Context: Our narratives depend upon us to linguistically create the whole story's huge sociological, historical, spiritual, natural environment. A context is also called the story's *situation*.

Continuity: A narrative has the inherent property of being continuous, representing time and space that shares occupancy in meaning. It asks for continuity, which means a series that represents a coherent whole, though it may present itself as broken, with its narrative problem being its need to fix itself and come back to its unbroken state.

In moviemaking, continuity is that written plan that details the succession and connection of scenes, one to the next, so their meaning renders narrative time in an order that makes sense.

Continuous beam: A plotting device that is borrowed from architectural engineering. The beam extends over more than two supports to develop the greatest rigidity and strength.

Every storyline will have a continuous beam of sufficient strength to figuratively carry it forward even in time that is not being actively portrayed. A child's growing up, for instance, does not have to be witnessed day by day but is assumed to transpire of itself along the continuous beam of this character's story.

Contrastive stress: The typographic means used to illustrate and emphasize spoken language. Heightening the meaning of a word or phrase—often via italics, boldface, or caps, this twentieth-century convention is often attributed to that *great* poet and *hearer of* the aMERikin *language*, Ezra Pound (emphasis mine).

Cooperative principle: Usually tacit but sometimes communicated directly through spoken or written guidelines, this is an agreement among participants who might include writer, narrator, the reader, and/or audience. The pact: to follow the same set of verbal conventions regarding usage, lexicon, diction, and grammar.

This principle is found particularly in matters of caretaker language, in which the narrator hovers over the reader seemingly to protect him or her from knowledge. The narrator also steers the reader through any writing about the harder subjects, such as sex, violence, and matters of the human body, about which the writer and reader agree to a certain level of aural shock and descriptive detail. (See **slang.**)

Copying: To learn how to write the visual elements of our narratives, we need to listen to what artists say about how they render likeness.

This is Edgar Degas on the notion of painting only what you see: "It is all very well to copy what you see, but it is much better to draw only what you still see in your memory. This is the transformation in which *the imagination collaborates with memory* [emphasis mine]. Then you only reproduce what has struck you, that is to say, the essential, and so your memories and your fantasy are freed from the tyranny that nature holds over them." (From "Souveniers sur Degas," in *Revenue Universally.*)

Correctness: This term has evolved into two meanings. The first that comes to mind is political correctness, which references our growing sensitivity—and countervailing reactions to this sensitivity—to the feelings of those who stand to the side of Dominant Culture. We get at what has made up Dominant Culture by glancing at the group portrait of Our Founding Fathers: tall, white, Protestant, presumably heterosexual men of Northern European ancestry. This matters to us as novelists in that the wish to be "politically correct" in our writing can force us to lie. It will also silence our characters' ability to realistically move, or think, or speak.

We work in the modern realist narrative tradition, which means we are interested in what the world *really is* rather than rainbows and unicorns. We all know this to be true: This is not a gender-neutral, color-blind world, equally accepting of every person of whatever race, religion, caste, class, age, ethnicity, or physical condition. Our society privileges the beautiful. We also privilege the athletic. I grew up in a family that thought smart people were usually "funny looking."

These are our own personal givens: It is up to each individual writer to face his or her own particular prejudices and to figure out how to use the tension they create to empower the narrative. You don't run from them, because we need exactly this kind of thing, as it is a source of interesting conflict.

A second sort of correctness also references a standard of language derived from the self-made rules of an institution, as published in its own respected publications. *The Chicago Manual of Style*, for instance, sets itself up and is accepted as the standard to which book publishing defers.

The issue of *correctness* in language usage is one we want to be aware of in order—often—to studiously ignore it, particularly when we're just setting out on the journey that feels like it wants to be longer narrative.

Correctness in language and usage is *always* defined by the group itself and does not exist empirically or objectively. A grandmother of mine who was a high school English teacher believed, however, that she knew what was and wasn't correct and poised like a hawk ready to flash down upon those of us romping and playing, like rodents, in the brush of my California childhood.

Correctness in matters of usage—and in matters of sensitivity to others who have felt left out of the American political process—are so often used as a way of asking those of us who would speak or write (we hope truthfully) to be quiet, to conform.

Very often the pedants and usage monitors are in recovery from their own feelings of linguistic inferiority. This is what informed my grandmother, who held in aural memory the sounds of her own dusty grandparents, who'd tramped two thousand miles west and were not properly educated—yet sought, as newly merchant-class white Western Americans, to sound and smell and look and *seem* correct in every way.

Political and linguistic correctness should feel as if it is material available for the novelist's use: that we, as Americans, work in the direction of inclusion of those who have traditionally been left out, that striving itself is a very American theme, striving for our betterment or trying to get from Here to There.

Correlation to our intuition about reality: Three tests measure where and how well our stories, our characters, and/or our elements of our plots lie within the Modern Realistic Tradition. First: Do they inspire our *sympathy*? Next: Do they inspire our *empathy*? Finally: Do these characters and their actions *correlate to our intuition about reality*? What this means is that the logic of these actions and reactions must be understandable to a majority of reasonable people, called the quorum.

Crisis: Crisis, marked at C on the diagram in the ABCs entry, is where narrative time catches up to the race of the story, then overtops it and speeds past it, no longer in pursuit. At this point plot, story, and the mechanics of narrative time converge, and the narrative tension reaches its pinnacle. The tension relaxes and lets gravity take hold. At this place the story suddenly seems to speed earthward, back toward its own sense of stability and resolution.

The ability of a narrative to ascend toward change is marked always by its own sense of gathering anticipation, driven by the story's ability to mirror the actual future as something that cannot be known, except as the force that pulls everything forward with its own sense of gravity.

A story moves always in the direction of the unpredictable, in that surprise and anticipation are what will bring the narrative its sense of being lifelike, as neither can be foretold.

D

Denouement (see also *falling action*): The short leg of the isosceles defines its *denouement*, or falling action, and must be equal in narrative weight to the two other longer sides or segments. The denouement stabilizes and balances the shape of the rest of the story, serving as its narrative sum. This leg contains, in its density, all the answers to the story's myriad questions. The final crisis will lie (in a manner almost mathematically predictable) three-fifths or four-fifths of the way in along the arc of the narrative, commencing at C, which is the point toward which all action rises. It is during the falling action that the meaning in a story will begin to *demonstrate* itself, finally allowing everything and everyone to announce what they really are.

Depth cues: We strive always, as novelists, to write in a manner that allows our readers to enter the scene. We want the narrative equivalent of the IMAX 3D experience, an enhanced sense of depth that the technology provides by what the film director James Cameron calls *depth cues*.

These are those sensory details that work to trick our visual cortex so that we no longer feel like we are outside the narrative's sense of its own three dimensions. We strive for intimacy with the sensory aspects of the episodes, furnished by the immediacy of details seen by the noticer and told to us by the narrator.

We come to depth cues, which let us feel that we've entered into the physical place where the narrative is ongoing, from what we've learned by living our lives in three dimensions. That is, we build our own by constantly processing both linear and aerial perspective.

In an interview with Terry Gross on National Public Radio, Cameron said, "What 3-D technology does is to provide us with sensory data that gives us parallax information; depth is being measured by the difference between what the left eye sees and what the right eye sees. This creates even more depth information, [and] all these different depth cues are correlated in the brain in the space of a few microseconds after first seeing the image. And, I would submit . . . the brain is more active, more engaged in the processing of the image."

What is successfully rendered in a good 3-D film is the sense that—as viewer—we haptically *occupy* the time and place, as a physical space, in which the narrative is occuring.

The written narrative is able to give depth cues, too. It dreams the story into being by tricking the visual cortex of the reader into working in synch with that of the narrator. The reader sees such a close approximation of what the noticer is seeing and what the narrator is reporting that we feel ourselves to inhabit the body of this noticer.

Some physical object—the Starbucks latte raised to your lips, its weight in your hands, its heat in your fingers, the smell of steamed milk hitting your face, the $4 or some equally ridiculous amount you've just shelled out for this drink—is often all that the noticer needs to feel incarnated, to be made flesh, within the narrative's scene.

We experience the timelessness and sense *of transportation* that we seek in dreams, a sense of depth of story that is alive and lying outside our thinking, figuring, rational minds, rivaled only by our night dreams.

As I wrote the scene in Part One in which Gigi sneaks into the Peterbilt cab, I felt myself surrounded by depth cues. There was the new car vinyl, the look of the miniaturized RV that a sleeper cab attains. To render this realistically, I watched an online sales video, which offered—no doubt—a very false sense of the cab's spaciousness. I gave her something to carry, the potted red geranium, which works as a talisman, or sacred object, that helps make a character feel real—though not to us, exactly. Giving them something to carry makes them real to themselves.

I suddenly really *liked* writing about the characters as soon as they began to develop their own physical presences, which came in part because of the physical things they owned: dog, potted flower, tricked-out truck cab.

It was suddenly fun to imagine this truly huge man and his little dog having their settled and tidy environment rattled by the chaos of one lightweight stowaway. The minute I arrived, via depth cues, in the cabin of the Peterbilt, I knew they'd come alive.

Destiny: One of the many ways in which fiction differs from life is fiction's tendency to carry an archaic sense of destiny. In a story, all the pieces matter—nothing, actually, is being left to chance, so its world is more orderly, finally, than the real one.

There is no actual residue or detritus of the day's events, as we have in real life. There is no true-life messiness, as a novel's every mess is a meaningful mess that is merely set dressing for a story's worldview. This worldview will finally become apparent when everything extraneous is cleared away—when all aspects, all characters, all events and incidents, even every bit of language, begins to shine with importance and meaning.

Dialect: Dialect is a language variety in which use of grammar, spelling (often inventive and/or phonetic), and vocabulary identifies it as regional. It will also often carry imports from another regional dialect or other native language that references the background of the user. The use of dialect among equals also calls out those to whom this language is addressed:

> Hey!
> Sup?
> You talking to me, girl?
> What he said.
> That.

Dialect, like any language that needs to be decoded, is full of hidden meaning, fraught with the unspoken freight of nuance. It is nuance—the barely seen chin lift accompanying the *Hey!*—that is almost always lost on the rest of us who stand outside this tight circle of intimate speech. It is nuance, that little hint or dance of meaning that might be said to give it the physical sense of the language, that was once called body English. It is an idiom that is being completely *inhabited* by the physical beings of its natives, while remaining largely unintelligible to the rest of us. Those speakers of other dialects in the same language can speak across dialects, but lose the richness of meaning.

Dialectic convergence: Dialectic convergence is the process of linguistic change in which dialects or accents meet, flirt, merge, marry, and become ever more like one another even as they strain to remain the same.

One geographic test I recently conducted yielded these results: The word *cater-corner*, or *catty-corner*, seems to have come into the American language as an import, through British English. It describes, say, two corners of a street—which from my earliest reckoning, I've called *kitty-corner*. The dialect convergence has moved it like this: The phrase originates in *quatre-*, or four-, cornered; then the notion of "diagonal" comes in to create *cater-corner* in the American South, then *catty-corner* in the Northeast, then *kitty-corner* as it moves west, toward me.

But usage is also very intensely *personal*: One man, someone I know very well, thought that any answer he gave was probably wrong. He said he'd call it any of those three things, depending on context, but that *kitty-corner* was probably the least correct answer, since it's what little children say.

Dialogue: Dialogue is the ability of the characters to advance the story by the act of speaking to one another, by the act of hearing one another, and by the act of hearing themselves speak.

Dialogue must earn its way into the story by its extreme likeness to the sound of actual speech. It must convince us that its words would be said by its characters—or it will register as prop language or as scene setting or maybe as an Information Delivery System devised by a writer who is trying to sneak an authorial intrusion past us. In that case it's probably better for the author to drop out of the narrative and the narrator's voice and address us in a footnote.

Before the plays of Aeschylus, all drama consisted of one actor declaiming his monologue—story was then in its telling, not showing, period, which is aural and nondramatic. But as soon as the second and third actors were introduced, the short plot was discarded for the one of greater complication. It now had a *larger compass*, in Aristotle's term.

Then Sophocles added scene painting, which acts to set our narratives down in *this specific* time and *this specific* place. Those in the audience seemed to be able to witness this reality right before their eyes. Suddenly, all the elements were in place for the modern narrative. It made its way to and through Shakespeare, going on to enrich our experience in both fiction and nonfiction;

in film; onstage; and in the excellence of the elaborated and ongoing narrative series developed for cable television and now on DVD for home viewing, available at a store near you.

Diction: Diction is the effective choice of words, especially those chosen by the poet or writer, and used to define a character in terms of caste/class, age, race or ethnicity, region, gender, age, language of origin, and many other variables.

We also use diction as a device to mimic what we think of as the idiom of a certain historical period. This includes the use or avoidance of such aural conventions as contractions—or the use or avoidance of what might be thought of as a hip, interruptive, or abbreviated style of speech. Characters will sometimes speak in full sentences, full stop, or seem to breathe long-windedly in and then just as long-windedly out. They can seem to run on and on, spouting paragraphs as if they were a bellows.

Your allowing your characters their own word choice, to say what they mean to say—but also to struggle, hem and haw and to *not* be able to speak up—is one of the more magical ways you'll find to bring them to life.

Dilemma in a plot: The character is presented with a *dilemma*; this dilemma worsens into *conflict*; conflict worsens into *crisis*;

crisis demands an *action*, which yields *reaction*, providing either a favorable or unfavorable outcome. Or—because all narrative is actually triangulated—it yields an outcome whose nature we cannot yet know.

Directionality: A shift happens at each narrative juncture, or hinge, that marks a shift in either the speed or direction of the story's *vectors* (see entry). Vectors are those arrows marking the angles of force and direction of each of the story's many elements, including each and every living character. That comprises all those who possess a chronology and are being acted upon by time. A vector also attends every place the story lights, in that place is marked and changed by time as well.

The directionality of the narrative will abruptly shift at the moment its climax is reached—when, as if in unison, all elements know they must come back to the line of action in order to resolve all conflicts. Everyone shows up, each plot piece now headed in the earthbound direction that will feel, to the story, like *home*.

le donnée: *Le donnée* is French for "the given." We get this from The Master, Henry James, on whom nothing was lost and who was extraordinarily concerned with class, status, property, all kinds of material possessions. James said we must simply acknowledge these elements as we place each character in what we might think of as his or her *situation*.

We've talked about this in terms of finding a character's backstory.

The donnée could be defined as what a story posits as its immutables, elements that cannot and will not change and are not exactly at issue. The given is also what James thought of as the writer's ideas. We might, more modernly, take these to be our own assumptions about caste/class, race or ethnicity, gender, age, sexual orientation, as these will serve to determine the ways in which our characters interact with society.

A novel's setting out to be a mystery or a romance and its operating by one or the other set of conventions is its donnée.

For most of us, what we think of as a story or character's givens can immediately chart the tension between our most basic human wish. We each want to be considered as ourself, in this one human body that we ever will inhabit, just as we are, as an individual, even as we try to sort out the degree to which we are simultaneously representative of those to whom we feel most akin.

The novel is very particularly about this kind of thing, those characters, like you and me, who want to set themselves apart as different from anyone who ever lived—even as they discover how much they are the same.

Here is some of what Henry James had to say:

> We must grant the artist his subject, his idea, what the French call his *donnée* [so] our criticism is applied only to what he makes of it.
>
> Naturally I do not mean that we are bound to like it or find it interesting: in case we do not our course is perfectly simple—to let it alone. We may believe that of a certain idea even the most sincere novelist can make nothing at all, and the event may perfectly justify our belief; but the failure will have been a failure to execute, and it is in the execution that the fatal weakness is recorded. If we pretend to respect the artist at all we must allow him his freedom of choice, in the face, in particular cases, of innumerable presumptions that the choice will not fructify. Art derives a considerable part of its beneficial exercise from flying in the face of presumptions, and some of the most interesting experiments of which it is capable are hidden in the bosom of common things. (From James's "The Art of Fiction.")

And it is Henry James who also tells us that the ". . . only reason for the existence of a novel is that it *does* compete with life."

Draft: Writing the longer narrative, in draft, through to its end is one of the greatest gifts a writer can give to herself. First drafts often have a messy, inchoate sense of self-discovery, which is exactly what you really do want to see—because it shows us all that this story is *alive*!

But remember: There will be *many* drafts, because there always are. This means a first draft deserves the right to *be really poorly written*, awful, completely incoherent, embarrassing, as this is where the story begins to teach itself to speak. There will be *many* drafts: this one, then another one, this is how it is always done.

You learn to write a book by writing a book: This is the only way the process *ever* works. You write it to learn how to write it, then you write it over again. You will probably write it once for its plot, once for its story, once for its subplot, once or twice for every character, once to nail it in temporal scene.

But, *hey*! This is great news! It means everything that's gone wrong so far will be more or less fixed when you get to draft ninety-nine.

Dramatic action: Dramatic action is the heart of the narrative, and we still need to get up each day and struggle to remember it. Representation of character is subordinate to the *actions* of the story—I'm sorry that I have to keep bringing this up.

Our characters remain tirelessly at the service of story, their job being to do the heavy lifting, to carry the story from scene to scene. This is the only way they get to be defined—by showing up and carrying out their own individual, perfectly existential actions.

This is why we give them the simple job of carrying some physical object as we struggle to make them feel real.

Dreaming the truth awake: Our stories strive to dream themselves awake, to be *like life*. If we do not believe in our own stories, as if they are a vivid dream, we ourselves remain unengaged. We are then concocting something that will never be art. Art demands that we enter the room of the narrative so our stories can become real to us. The word for this achievement is *verisimilitude*, from the Latin for "simulating the truth."

Duration: *Internal duration* is the term we use to measure the length of an episode. *External duration* refers to the more objectively measured segments of time, such as an hour or day or week. You will assign every episode both an internal and an external duration. You will do this *eventually*, while striving to leave the story's time sense fluid, flowing out to include what only it now knows it must include.

Internal duration refers to that sense of time that will eventually establish itself within the story's walls and will tick away with the same assuredness and regularity as a heartbeat if you allow the story a subjective sense of its interior metronome.

Dynamic verbs: Dynamic verbs are those verbs, or words of action, that express activities and changes of state, allowing complications to arise as the characters move naturally in the direction of crisis along the line of action. In doubt about whether your character has anything dynamic and physical going on? Give him or her something to carry.

E

Earning in: Everything in your book must earn in, prove its right to exist. This test allows for and proves artistic unity. I don't know exactly where or when Aristotle said this but I am almost entirely sure that he did indeed say it. So here, at least, it earns in.

Echo utterance: We repeat one another. This is how we learn to talk. We repeat one another, and we repeat ourselves. An echo utterance is a type of spoken language that repeats, in whole or in part, what's just been said by another speaker, often with contrasting, ironic, or contradictory meaning.

"How old are you?" Bob asks.

"Nineteen," Gigi says.

He says nothing, as this does not deserve the courtesy of response.

"Seventeen," she says.

"Seventeen?"

"Well, not quite," she says. "Sixteen, till I get to my next birthday."

"*Sixteen?*" Bob asks. "*SIX-teen?*"

"Well, maybe not exactly," she says.

Economy, narrative: One of the principles of artistic unity, whereby everything that does not add to the speed and direction of the story must—eventually, if not exactly now—go.

Effects and their causes: Placing an effect along the line of the story, then writing to discover its cause, is one of the many tools the writer of the longer narrative employs. It deepens the mystery and creates suspense in plotting. The device dates at least from Horace, who named the way we can begin a story *in medias* *res,* or plunk in the middle of dramatic affairs, as if we've been *snatched*—and this is Horace's own excellent word—to the heart of the action, then left to unravel how we arrived there.

Elision: The American language moves in the direction of haste. For this reason we will regularly omit sounds in spoken language, saying *icetea* for iced tea or *baconneggs* for bacon and eggs.

Capturing this sense of elision helps the writer get to the quickness with which urban people deal with spoken language. Even those whose speech patterns are deliberate and slow work with elision, dropping syllables from the center of a word as it becomes worn and familiar.

We all say words, particularly place names, familiarly, in a manner that makes them sound like they belong to us.

Ellipsis: Ellipsis is the omission of part of a structural whole— sentence, paragraph, speech, or scene—for reasons of emphasis or economy. It's invaluable in creating the texture of everyday speech of our characters.

> "*SIX-teen?*" Bob asks.
> "Well, I . . . ?" Gigi looks away, unable to meet his gaze.

Embedded memory: This memory is of the less-than-a-flashback variety. In it, a narrator's thought process is perfectly traced. We can therefore see—aha!—that this antecedent action, an event or incident, meets the character in such a way that a memory, in scene, is brought to mind, in the manner of free association (see **impacted memory**).

Empathy: This is a test to which our characters and the events that befall them must be put. If they fail the empathy test, they do not "*earn in*" (see entry) to our stories. Empathy asks that we feel with a character; if we do, we enter the three-dimensional sense of the narrative space in which the dramatic capture of events is occurring. What this asks is that we feel as if we are participating in a character's feelings.

That we *feel with* Bigger Thomas, as he becomes a murderer, proves the greatness of Richard Wright's *Native Son*.

The word *empathy* derives from the Greek for "affection," something that may be entirely lacking when our feelings of *sympathy* are provoked. When we feel bonded to a character, we are physically *identifying* with him or her, in that our bodies experience this character's fear, terror, inexplicable rage. Bigger Thomas is young, poor, male, badly educated, African American—none of which I am, yet as I read the book, through the power of empathy, I *become* him.

Energy, narrative: Any temporary pause will power the story. It does this by consolidating energy needed to move the narrative into the story's future, closer to its resolution. All narrative conflict, all pauses and rests, will lie either along the story's arc or be placed along its narrative tributaries. These energies contribute to the storyline rather than angle away from it.

Each engagement with risk, each revelation, each change, each meaningful event and incident and action contributes its energy to the sum of the story's narrative power. Each element also composes itself to figuratively match the shape of the larger narrative. Every narrative piece will be made of triangulating angles that subtly echo the storyline in sound and feel—or your pacing, plot, and tension.

Engineering: Engineering is the art and science of applying scientific principles to practical ends in designing and constructing systems of narrative.

The most common way of describing a system of narrative is by naming its genre: romance, mystery, memoir, thriller. This is shorthand, but it helps narrow our task: Many types of stories already have a very distinct sense of their own narrative engineering, which we must study if we want to write one successfully.

Epiphany: This thought action derives from the Greek term for "a showing forth," used to mean the sudden realization or comprehension of the meaning of something in drama. James Joyce revivified it early in the last century, by allowing his character Stephen Dedalus to arrive in the place where narrative meaning is apprehended. This is the modern sense of the word, in which a character comes to an understanding of some larger narrative meaning, this meaning—which applies to the narrative whole—deriving from his or her apprehension of a single part.

Episode: Fictional time is described and measured by the episode. It is the three-dimensional feeling that pieces of story take on—and from which every block of effective narrative is built.

In the episode, the writer cedes the storytelling to the narrator, who enters the scene and knows all there is to know about this scene. The narrator causes this piece of narrative time and space to come alive in the reader's mind, in the manner of a dream.

A novel is actually made of its episodes, these short, entirely manageable narrative elements. That a novel is made by a writer's writing its episodes is the most liberating notion I came across as I was setting out to become a novelist. Not only *can* we write a book this way; it is *the only way* that books are ever written.

Equality between writer and reader: "Ungenerous fiction," writes the novelist John Gardner, is "first and foremost a fiction in which the writer is unwilling to take the reader on as an equal partner."

We are to assume nothing more than that our readers are like we are—as interested as we are in what we're interested in, as smart as we are, and just as well spoken. If we do happen to speak a couple of more languages than our readers do, we gracefully translate so they get the impression that they speak a couple of languages, too.

We do not write down to our readers, because we are not better than they are. This pertains especially when we're writing for young people; we are not *better* than children and don't even necessarily know more than they do. We are merely older.

Think of Shakespeare, who wrote generously and for the illiterate masses. Write to Shakespeare, telling Will everything your heart contains. I promise you: He's heard all of this. Will will totally *get* you.

Etymological fallacy: The attitude that the earlier, preferably old-est and most codified, meaning of a word is also the most correct. This attitude is fallacious. It is also reactionary.

It is a fallacy because it's false. What is true about language always and inevitably, and what is particularly true of the American language, is that it is always changing. This is because our language is alive. Its words are, therefore, *always* modifying and migrating through common usage. That's how they develop multiple meanings. These meanings can *all* be correct, even when they contradict one another.

Let's take a term currently in the gray anteroom of what words *used to* correctly mean and still ought to according to the etymological fallacy.

The word *peruse*, is frankly—and not to be mean here, but honestly?—just entirely confused. Half the reading-writing pop-ulation believes it to still mean what it used to mean, which is "to read with great care." The other half of any sampling of reading-writing people believe it means "to read over hastily," "to skim."

So because all of this submits to majority rule, the word's on its way OUT of actual usefulness. A word cannot be meaningful unless it does a little work on its own behalf.

This is how I'd use the word *peruse* if I had to: I'd have two reading-writing characters—and these are the characters I tend to write—arguing over how the word should be used.

Because it is basically a stupid word, in that it's posturing and snobbish-sounding. The American language privileges the use of words that are direct and plainspoken: If you mean "read something carefully" why not say "read something carefully"? Better yet, have your characters enact something's being read really carefully, which takes all kinds of narrative time.

Euphemism: A euphemism is the substitution of a vague term for a highly specific one, in the hope that the vaguer one might be more socially appropriate, less offensive, and/or cooperatively agreed upon. We care about the use of euphemisms because we're working in the American language, which is rife with slang that is rife with vulgarity. We also operate within a societal matrix that asks us to be genteel, as this shows we know the context in which we're speaking.

Evil: In fiction, being bad is more interesting than goodness can ever organize itself to be. Goodness is more admirable and less abundant in our world, except when we find it twinned with what we might think of as naturalness.

As humans we are ceaselessly interested in our temptations to evil. These derive partly from our memory of ourselves in the freedom of our own lawlessness—back before the moments of language, when we were just dropping the spoon over and over again to see if it would reappear.

What bifurcated us was the act of naming ourselves, of distinguishing ourselves from the beasts, which gave us this tragic state of self-consciousness.

In making our characters we hope to find the flaw in the cloth. Many of these flaws conform more or less to the Seven Deadly Sins, from which most of us are so bifurcated that we can no longer enumerate them.

Fiction offers us solace from our own recognition of evil, saying we are not alone in our greed, our envy, what some might call our Tiger Woods–like covetousness—that we want not only our own wife but this showgirl and that cocktail waitress, too.

Stories tell us we are not alone and sometimes offer hints about what to do about our own imperfections.

Evil, as a component of character, is a very dense molecular material, much more dangerous and singular than the more commonly found *lack of good*. Most human-feeling characters are an admixture of good and the lack of good. For true evil, see Shakespeare's Iago, or Cormac McCarthy's Chigurh in *No Country for Old Men*.

Exaggeration: We are fiction writers, and we will use exaggeration for effect. We will use it thematically, making the character of Bob, the trucker, larger than he probably needs to be because we want him to stand for certain very solid and physical aspects. We also want his hugeness to contrast with the electron weightlessness of Gigi.

"You must boldly exaggerate the effects of either harmony or discord," the painter Sonia Delaunay tells us, speaking of colors. "Accurate drawing, accurate color," she goes on, "is perhaps not the essential thing . . . " We are interested in the painting rather than the photograph.

Explanation: We try our best to avoid the kind of overarching language about our work that seeks to sum it up or explain it. The explanations will always be too simple, will always fail—if we could explain what this book of ours wants to say, we'd have no real motive for writing it.

"When an artist explains," as the sculptor Alexander Calder tells us, he or she will need to "either scrap what he has explained, or make his subsequent work fit in with his explanation. *Theories* may be all very well for the artist [but] shouldn't be broadcast to other people."

Expletive [deleted]: An exclamatory word or phrase, usually thought to be obscene, blasphemous, or profane—and nearly always referencing either God, Satan, the parts of the human body or any of their myriad bodily functions—that seems to both fascinate and shame us.

F

Fairy tales: In a fairy tale, there's no question that the character will act in character, because fairy tale characters are invented to be predictable. What we like about them is that these characters cannot and do not change. They seem stamped out, repetitive, as if hatched in the Creature Shop, a kind of sweatshop assembly line producing masses of gnomes and witches and unicorns but never individuals, whose futures, like our own, can simply never be foretold in a fairy tale structure.

We cannot know the future. The future humbles us, or should humble us. How can we know that we—along with our husband—will on a clear summer's evening, be hit by a car while crossing the street in a crosswalk? While turned to one another to discuss *gelato*? While walking exactly as we've walked maybe a hundred times before?

The future is inventive. It doesn't happen to be made by butterfly wings or to be fabricated in the Creature Shop by characters whose outsides always *exactly* match their insides so they lack *any* surprise. It's the predictability in any genre—romance or spy story or mystery or fairy story or novel by William Makepeace Thackeray—that offers us either comfort or fails to finally bring us along because it lacks surprise. We both do and do not want both comfort and surprise in what we write and what we read, and maybe in almost equal proportions.

So the best books are both surprising and resonant. They carry elements of the whole history of narrative—that same old river that arrives to power our mill race—yet feel almost entirely new. They feel as if an invented language has evolved in which to sing this oddly familiar tune. Our books do absolutely stand in the lineage of those that have come before them, so—though we do not learn to write by copying other writers—writing actually can and should teach us how to read.

We don't, as adults, usually want to read the story in which ugly people are bad, pretty people are good, all young people are juvenile delinquents and old women are hags and witches and crones with horrible cackling voices. We want the characters who will fight for their individuality, who mutiny, who work against type, who *insist* on this or that. We want those characters to cast off their old costumes, to be individuals if even to spite us, their Authors.

Fairy tales are told almost entirely in *ambient time* (see entry). That's why the child hearing them feels protected from what might otherwise seem like terribly realistic creatures and horrible events: deaths of parents, human-to-animal transformations, cannibalism, immolation. It is in the nature of the fairy tale to promise that everyone lives happily ever after, which children hear in the kind of time they are being told, which is circular.

The circular telling relieves the fairy tale of having to climb the arc of narrative. There are adult fairy tales, too, including romances and certain kinds of more sophisticated women's literature where the happy ending—this is always rendered as marrying the perfect man—is guaranteed.

The fairy tale's circular logic, whose affective sign is that it is *comforting*, lacks the third rail of *risk* that powers the traditional narrative in the direction of the unknown.

If the narrative written in the Modern Realistic Tradition is the roller coaster thrill ride, then the fairy tale is the merry-go-round, which might have a monster or gargoyle hidden among its painted horses but is a ride nearly everyone learns to take without being fearful.

We are taught, from childhood, to be so at home in the fable that the prospect of happily-ever-after is a costume we happily dress up in as we step out of the house on a Friday night. Even the most modern of narratives borrows from this the happily-ever-after conceit, that sense of timelessness, which may be felt as almost misremembered or nostalgic. James Salter's masterly story "American Express" begins in a dreamy, generalized time that feels as if it's being witnessed through the half-remembered, golden blur of inexactitude, the Olden Days.

Falling action (see also *denouement*): Beyond the apex of the story's crisis no new characters may be introduced, no new problems or complications may arise (except as a subset of problems and complications inherent in the story all along). Disguises are taken off and transformations are either finished or undone, as the good that has been masquerading as evil—or the other way around—is revealed for what it really is.

The story turns toward home, now working to tie up all the loose ends that have been unraveled by its telling, the story now dramatically changing in directionality, power, and speed. After this last turn a sense of culmination attends, as if narrative time is being compacted, growing shorter. The story's pace very naturally quickens as it begins to hurry toward resolution. It's as if everything is now rushing to meet its destiny, all action being taken over in an ever-narrowing sense of its own inevitability, as if right around the corner The End will suddenly be at hand.

This shift in both speed and direction of all the story's vectors—those angles of ascent and descent upon which the plot has been built—will echo at the C of each and every episode (or compilation of episodes) as if to let these resolutions speak across the peaks to one another. Minor resolutions also move in a manner allowing them to thematically point onward toward the apex of the tallest peak, which is where we will find the crisis/resolution of the story as a whole.

Fantasy: As one of E. M. Forster's invaluable *Aspects of the Novel* (there are seven), fantasy plays its part as a motive in the writing of even the most realistic narrative. It's in the charmed circles of our stories that the past finally reveals itself to us and the future can be discerned, the lost are given back to us, and Beginning and End are made to meet.

Flashback: The mechanism by which the flashback is used in narrative mirrors the way memories are physically triggered as thought actions. That is, we will startlingly and involuntarily remember something because of an action or event occuring in the present time. The involuntary nature of memory is what imbues the scenes our minds remember with their sense of surprise and discovery. We seem to come upon an older memory as if experiencing it for the first time because it is only now that we understand what it contextually means.

This triggering event is called the *antecedent action* (see entry). The link between what is experienced in the present time and the content of the memory must be *logically apparent* as the episode in flashback plays out.

The flashback, when used properly, will *always* have this supremely logical link, in that an association has been made in the mind of a character that triggers this one specific memory.

The cause-and-effect relationship of these linkages is proved over and over again: Because I lived the unspooling time of the flashback, I came to know the answer to the question. A flashback is not, however, a vague gesture by the narrator or the author—often seen in an intrusion—in the direction of the narrative past, used to import some items of information or background.

Force (see also *vector*): A force is something within a plot that exerts an influence on a character that, in turn, tends to produce a change in the direction of the action. The vector is used to describe this force: This is the fatter, thinner, longer, shorter arrow of directionality that describes any character or event able to import change to the narrative.

Forces lie both within and outside a character; these energies can be marked, in plotting with this directional arrow. Its width and length illustrate strength.

A vector may also be used to mark external events as they meet a character's internal motivations, as he is forced to move through conflict by choosing a specific course of action.

Fractal nature of the narrative: A story resembles a mountain in its regular irregularity. A story grows by its own similarly shaped increments: These are its episodes. This is to say it will have the feeling of evolving rather than of being manufactured—that of the conch shell or leaf rather than of the car being mass-produced on the assembly line.

Its orderly disorderliness derives from the narrative's wish to be taken as *lifelike*, something found in nature, while leading upward to the mountain's highest peak. It avoids climbing, say, the pyramid, whose shape is bilateral, regular, manmade, and therefore predictable.

The predictable story collapses into knowable parts, halves or quarters, and defeats itself. Its mathematics and internal geometries ask for the story to work in thirds or fifths, to turn away from regularity in the direction of what will feel like its own life force. A story develops according to the regularly irregular forms familiar to us from nature because it is trying to convince us of its correlation with reality, its natural affinity for The Truth.

Free will: Characters may seem to stumble around in our stories almost as a matter of coincidence, with the *arrows of time* (see entry) rushing at them and by them as if these characters aren't paying that much attention. This immediately changes as they intersect the line of action, where *something begins to happen.*

It may occur to you that your characters become more and more pushed down and positioned as subordinates to plot, that the story begins to reach up, grab them, and ring them in, no matter how hard they try to twist away. This occurs because—unlike in real life—a story happens *to* a character until it starts to happen *because* of a character. The degree to which our characters will or will not prove to be victims of their own circumstances is one of the great subjects of any literature.

We are born. We come trailing all of this stuff that tries to determine us. Henry James calls it *le donnée* (see entry), our given, and it gives our characters the situations that put them in flux, at sea.

Matters that fall within the vector of the given are determined by genetics, by birthright, by class or caste or background, by ethnicity, by language of origin. These are then, in combination, made almost insanely complex by society's pluses and minuses—which set the angles for each of us as we start life's trudge.

The more class-driven and class-determinant societies expect that these vectors say more about a character's *character*. Americans, however, tend to want other notions to determine the content of the heart and soul. We've been taught to believe that we are not prisoners of history, that history is what we're making with our own existential actions. Therefore we, as writers, would especially like to give our characters this capability of free will.

So we posit the element of choice whenever we set out to write the longer narrative, because this gives our characters the chance to move into the future and to change in ways that surprise not only us but the characters themselves.

If you have no character who, so far, seems capable of choice, you are, so far, working solely with flat characters. You're going to have to go shopping to put some psychological meat on them.

The Future: E. M. Forster—in his ever-helpful *Aspects of the Novel*—calls a story's ability to read its own future the power of prophecy.

Forster imagines that all good books contain it, that the story is looking for something off there in the novel's future, something that pulls the characters toward it with such magnetized power that it feels like *fate*. This means that when a character comes to a crossroads, he seems to be picking the right road—or the wrong road, as the plot decrees—but his choice is actually inevitable. The Gods of Plot will not let him choose otherwise.

A character is welded to the story's need to spin itself outward, moving toward the swirling inevitability that picks up the threads of your every character's fate or destiny. It then delivers them all to the place where they heat up, come closer, and become more molecularly dense. This is where they become most exactly and essentially themselves: The Future.

G

Genre: This is a French word meaning "category" or "type." It helps you define the neighborhood in which you're building this house of yours; we have different expectations of a book according to its genre.

A thriller or mystery will be made according to stricter rules, a more formulaic structure, than will books in other genres. So, too, will the romance, which demands a particular ending.

The one rule for the novelist is that you become acquainted with the genre in which you hope to work by reading the best writers in it.

Gesture: As writers we can learn so much by listening to what visual artists say about their craft. Leonardo da Vinci suggests that we study the movements of the deaf—that the eloquence of their actions can say so much more than words, which we all know to be inexact.

The deaf use gesture, as he reminds us, that can be *seen in action*. *Spoken* language will try to get at same thought, but it comes as something translated from its original, more vehement expression.

As writers we are always noticing and interpreting gesture, those very nuanced actions of our characters who are telling us, without speech, what they are thinking and feeling. The fact that this lies below language allows our characters to say in gesture what they cannot—for whatever reason—know well enough yet to have found the language to say.

Plot, as we struggle to remember, hides what the story strives to show. Our characters' gestures sometimes allow them to do both things at once.

H

Haptic, or bodily, senses: Essential to the narrative, the haptic senses offer the reader the ability to enter the scene, using the physical presence of the character—who experiences the hot, cold, wet, dry, smoky, steamy environment in which the story's scenes are playing out. It is through the realm of haptic perception that we, by proxy, interact with the physical parts of the narrative, where objects feel weighted and three-dimensionally solid.

I

Impacted memory: The writer places this kind of memory down within the context of a scene. A character—in the real time of this scene—can then seem to leave its physical time and place to vividly recall another time and place. The character is prompted to remember something as a thought action. An impacted memory may seem to want to be a flashback. Unlike a flashback, however, the impacted memory stays in the mind of the character who is doing the remembering. This memory doesn't assume an episodic form, where it would be seen in scene, like a flashback.

Instead, the character stands and remembers within the context of the original scene. If used in a skillful way, we can learn a great deal: that the character cannot help thinking this thought, which may feel compulsory. In less-than-skillful hands, we begin to worry about the logistics of this memory: that it is actually telling us something new, that it isn't being used to import background. We worry about how much time it takes to remember something and how much detail is given to this memory.

The memory is *impacted* because there is no outlet; it doesn't allow the character to leave the scene and be transported to another time and place. This sense of the character's being trapped within the impacted memory might be used for powerful effect, in painting a character within the thought action that must be revisited and may well feel inescapable. (See **embedded memory**.)

Ingots of time: You write an episode. You write another one. The two don't need to sit next to each other in Time and Space. You trust the story to tell you later what will form the bonds between the incidents. You're discovering the simplest thing about writing a novel: that it's built of pieces of discrete episodic time, pieces that might resemble Lego blocks. They can be lifted, interlocked, sorted, scattered, reshaped, stacked by color, stacked by shape or size. An ingot of time—the phrase comes from Eudora Welty—can be described as the amount of narrative time it takes for its action to come to its own sense of completion.

Invented language: Those of us working in the American language have at our hands an invented language of majestic proportions, almost infinitely detailed and rich in idiom, connotation, denotation, bawdy vulgarity, astonishingly musical and humorous slang. We hear language change, even as we speak it, every day of our lives. So we understand that we, as writers, are perfectly capable of inventing language whenever we find it necessary.

I write both fiction and nonfiction and therefore try very hard to pinpoint *exactly* the use of particular words and phrases, which is a way of entering the narrative space at the moment of that particular expression.

Every one of us, in fiction and nonfiction, is inventing language as we write, because we are deliberately and specifically sorting—choosing to include or exclude—the grunts, the hums, the starts and stops, the infelicities with which we actually humanly speak.

For the film *Avatar*, the linguist Paul Frommer, of the University of Southern California, helped director James Cameron create the characters' planetary language, which eventually had a vocabulary of twelve hundred words. It was coached to the actors so they'd speak with a consistent accent; it has a syntax, a grammar, which borrows from German, with the verb placed at the end of the sentence. Because it follows fairly strict linguistic rules, it sounds "correct," even though we couldn't possibly translate it.

We do the same thing in creating these worlds of ours, these places that want to have the *this*-ness and physical and temporal specificity that says they are sufficiently round and heavy to have earned their own linguistic gravity.

Time and place matter so much to the novelist; nothing expresses their narrative intersection as well as our use of language.

It occurs to me that a draft of a novel is always devoted to an accumulation of language—as if it takes the draft to invent the lexicon with which you will write.

K

Kaleidoscopic aspects: These are the six basic ways we are allowed into the narrative space: time, tense, tone, person, perspective, point of view. They are kaleidoscopic because they work together in a shifting and prismatic fashion to engage us within the story's rooms of time. We dial ourselves into these narrative spaces of ours; we also dial ourselves out and away. We do this constantly, arranging for our noticer to have the best vantage point for witnessing the scene's action.

The writer who feels he or she is somehow boxed in, in a dark closet peeking out or in some tight and unpromising corner, need only change one of these aspects to feel the entire scene shift and morph.

These elements are *intricately* interrelated. A shift in perspective—say, moving up and away from an intimate third into a more lofty or omniscient third person—will immediately and profoundly change the *tone* of your writing. You will now look down on the room of time from an emotional remove.

L

Length: A novel can be almost any length. It is unrestricted; it will measure itself out in whatever number of episodes it needs to accomplish its own goals. The length of the longer narrative is whatever is required for its hero to pass through a series of probable or necessary stages from misfortune to happiness, or from happiness to misfortune. That it has no set length is one of the more magical properties of the novel: It is *exactly* self-delimiting.

Likeness: A likeness is pleasing to the reader because it seems to capture the spirit of an event or the soul of an individual. It therefore preserves this person or event toward immortality.

Both comedy and tragedy depend on likeness and our need to recognize the reality of a character or event. Comedy, however, will emphasize the broader, more generalized aspects and may work more successfully with the flatter characters, who do less to rise up and resist the bonds of typecasting. Likeness works *against* type, in that working toward likeness asks how this individual *is* an individual.

Tragedy depends upon our understanding whatever *specific* sadness and loss has happened to this particular individual versus Loss, written large, in its most general sense. The narrative arts work toward individuality, in likeness, to import this specificity. Since this particular character matters, we think, we each, as individuals, matter too.

Line of action: The line of action describes the plot as it works with story to move events in a causal manner from one meaningful incident to the next. It is a line of indefinite length, because we allow a novel to take as long as it needs to arrive at its own resolution.

Looks of our characters: We want to capture the looks of our characters through an accumulation of detail, as happens in real life. You don't freeze-frame in real life; you don't absorb the mug shot specs of physical attributes. Instead we come upon living characters as seen in gesture, in which their bodies, their faces, their hair, their fingers, their arms and legs are actively moving, as they do things that show they are alive.

We aren't particularly convinced by Department of Motor Vehicle stats—height, weight, race, hair color, eye color—which have the immediate sense of complete inexactitude.

We apprehend people's looks comparatively. Physicality in a novel is therefore best rendered through relative description. So-and-So is bigger than Someone Else, as Bob is larger than Gigi, who is so small she has been overlooked in her sketchy past.

M

Magic, ritual, and charms: A sense of magic hovers around the triangulated elements of the longer narrative, and storytelling magic brings belief to this work we do. Indeed, *abracadabra* is similar to the Aramaic word for "I will create as I speak." Those of us who live and breathe in this strange novelistic world of the waking dream may, indeed, be superstitious people who are trying to dream ourselves awake, out of the reality of the day-to-day.

We're in good and ancient company, as mankind has sought to throw a net made of words around all of Elaborated Creation— ever since the first moments we found the words to begin talking about all this.

Meaning: Any serious novel must render its actions and events into a sense of meaning. The work of plot and story weave together along the warp and woof of meaning; it is what makes everything in a novel adhere. Every scene in a book lasts only long enough for it to proclaim its meaning. The novel itself then lasts only long enough for all its elements to show what they mean to one another.

Every element of these books of ours will—if not now, then eventually—be sharply seen in the bright light of their own meaning. This does not demand that everything in a book become reductively explicable. For instance, a character like Chigurh in Cormac McCarthy's brilliant novel *No Country for Old Men* is purely evil, with no explanation ever given as to what has caused him to be evil. We are taught the meaning of this character by the book, which is that pure evil does, in fact, exist.

Melodrama: Characterized by the manipulation of character types and by extreme emotions and situations, melodrama results when sympathy, empathy, or our intuition about reality deserts our work. We are left with elements of plot that have come unhinged from believability.

A hero will be unambiguously and uninterestingly good, a villain thinly and uncomplicatedly bad. Nothing will diverge much from type or expectation. We come upon no real surprises or subtlety.

As we write early drafts of dramatic events, the characters and events may well seem melodramatic, because we haven't yet had the chance to write them down *into scene* and away from the formulaic.

As a story and its scenes become more and more themselves, they shed their more primitive and melodramatic impulses.

Memory: This is an essential element in solving a novel's mysteries. The mind of the book will eventually seem to hold all its various elements in one coherent and compelling act of narrative memory. All its questions of Cause and Effect, After and Before, motivation and sequence, will be solved.

The reader is constantly being asked to add to this sense of cumulative memory, as the book's meaning compounds.

Memory, as such, is one of our most important narrative tools and materials. It is also tricky to work with and easy to abuse. Memories—when squandered on characters who sit around gazing into mirrors pondering this or that—quickly become tiresome. And we all must resist building something as structurally large as a novel on the shifting sands of a character who is allowed indulgent memories. We know, after all, the trap of memory: It is unreliable at best and misleading at worst.

We worry about our characters' memories because we know about our own. We worry, too, about memory as the kind of thought action that sits within a scene and takes up narrative time without giving us much in return. We want it to work as every action must—to import to the narrative an opportunity for change.

One way of viewing memory as an active narrative component: Assign it a vector, and ask that a character's thinking *this thing* will somehow change the course of the story.

This means it matters, that the character used to think *this*, but events have *changed* what he or she thinks, so now the character thinks *that*, which takes the form of *epiphany* or *revelation*.

Metafictional techniques: Metafiction is the kind of writing that takes for its subject the mere fact that it is being written. An immediate example of metafictional technique occurs in this book, in Part One's elaborated story of Bob, the trucker and his soon-to-be-adopted daughter, Gigi. This narrative has been developed in Part One's chapters as a tool—to illustrate the many aspects of the storytelling process.

When you're lucky, your metafictional creations begin to assert themselves, in wanting to become as real as the next character in fiction. This is the narrative's better nature, asking you and me to stop being clever and get on with the work at hand. Metafictional techniques have been with us since Chaucer. The first novel whose own writing was used as a narrative subject is *The Life and Opinions of Tristram Shandy, Gentleman*, published in England in 1759.

The actual term *metafiction*, however, derives from a particular kind of twentieth-century work in American and European expression that takes as its subject fictional writing and its conventions. It is characterized by an ironic, knowing tone and extreme self-consciousness. This can irritate the reader, who just wants the writer to be quiet, starting right about *now*, and to start inventing a plausible dream, an escape.

The metafictionalist keeps everyone—including himself or herself—at a distance from narrative belief. We tire of the writer who must continually reference himself: *Lookit! Author as maker!*

The writer working in the Modern Realistic Tradition hopes that these metafictional creations will fight back, rise up, win. We hope for them to begin to feel real, which occurs as soon as we get our ham-fisted, manipulative hands off them.

They stop being *our* creations and begin to belong to themselves, as my own characters have begun to do. When I stumbled upon the name *Gigi* written with stars in her name in the stall of an imaginary bathroom, I had one kind of narrative in mind. Its landscape was Edward Hopper–esque and bleak; it reverberated with profound cynicism and loneliness. Gigi was one of the hopeless cases, I thought, with nowhere to go but down.

I had no idea my story would come up with this sweet-natured, oversized trucker whose wife is dead, whose kids are grown and gone, who has a Chihuahua mix named Diego, and who has, evidently, just happened upon the fourteen-year-old girl, in foster care, whom he'll end up adopting.

And, yes, you will want your characters to be *exactly* this defiant and self-inventive.

Mind of the book: The book has agency to know what you and I cannot yet know about the book we're writing. The mind of the book holds all of its story; understands the workings of its plot; and feels, without having to ever learn, what must be included and what must be left out.

The mind of the book does the book's balancing, its narrative juggling, its hiding and revealing, its adding and subtracting.

It is the agency that furnishes stage directions that has So-and-So enter exactly *now*.

A story, if it's good and instructive and amusing, will go places we didn't know we wanted to go (and may, more than likely, have dreaded being led). The only predictive aspect of a good book is its capacity to surprise its own writer.

The mind of the book—which exists, unseen and unheard, in the unconscious—knows that we're often afraid of the simplest things, that we might be caught accidentally telling the truth instead of saying what we think we ought to say, which is always spouting a piece of language that is *received*.

So we'll set up ways by which we ignore the mind of the book. We hope to keep our stories safe, but we make them tame—by, for instance, mapping the entire territory before we allow our narrative explorers to tread there. Mapping, charting, making an outline or timeline or other kind of chronological order disrespects a story's NOW. This NOW wants to engage the reader with the immediacy of the senses. This means we, as our story's writers, must be brave enough to go to that place ourselves.

An action, if *allowed* to enact itself, will very naturally unfold. This will become effortless, since action is what your story's made of. A story has a nature that is both active and direct. The writing is like expert testimony of the best eyewitness. We vividly *see* the scene, hear the characters as they speak their lines of dialogue. An episode's events will be *seen*, *heard*, and also haptically *witnessed*. They will be *felt* with all the knowledge our human bodies have at their disposal.

Modern Realistic Narrative Tradition: The critic James Wood has termed our tradition, inherited from Gustave Flaubert, *modern realistic narration*. Flaubert was reacting against his own soft-focused romantic inclinations. He was trying to write the harsh truth of the world's realities, not the gauzy one that echoes the neoplatonic notions of a perfection that is attainable on earth in certain kinds of love.

The narrator is able to share consciousness with any character who is needed. Flaubert invented this as he was writing *Madame Bovary*, a revolution in the use of point of view on a magnitude of the Theory of Relativity.

Moment: A moment is not only the Now of the narrative instant. It also—via the term's use in architecture—marks the tendency of a force to produce the rotation of a body about a point or line, the movement equal in magnitude of the force.

Moment, in narrative mechanics, is another way of describing *the crisis that allows the story to turn and move on.* The reason we need a term for this is that it recognizes the resistance any narrative object offers to a change in its direction. The term *moment* also refers to a sense of magnitude or narrative importance.

Mystery: Every good novel is a mystery. The longer narrative—more than any other form of art—acknowledges and seeks to encapsulate what we can truly know about our relationship to existence.

The mystery says: We simply cannot know.

The genre of the mystery is exciting because it posits a case in which every aspect of the narrative is complexly hidden—and then, point by point, resolved.

The well-made mystery is a pleasure to read because the writer has gone to such effort to match every element to its own hidden solution, like the perfect clockwork that plot can become in skillful hands. Every writer of the longer narrative should study the form of the classic mystery to see the beautiful machine of plot in action.

The rest of us also incorporate huge territories of what cannot yet be known in our longer narratives. The novel accounts for learning what is at first hidden from view by allowing for the passage of Time. Along the way characters will share with the writer and, by extension, with the reader what John Gardner calls "[A]n increasingly moving series of recognitions or moments of under-standing." These are not exactly *Aha! Fooled you!* surprises. They are moments that affirm what we had already suspected.

Both writer and reader seem to come to these moments of recognition together, so the reader is swept up into the writer's satisfaction at having the mystery resolved.

This is the pocket in time that holds both the question of why and its answer. All time encapsulated within this pocket is made vivid and significant by the tension of the questions being posed.

N

Narrative arc: This is the Line of the Story as it moves the actions upward in the direction of conflict. Individual episodes also follow the pattern. They move in direction of crisis, after which narrative time skips ahead to the next scene, in which the story can be seen in action.

Narrative hinge: A scene or episode will very naturally move toward the link to the next scene in which the events cannot be accurately predicted. Crisis provides that link, that place for a narrative to *hinge*. A narrative hinge is positioned at the point where the angle or direction of the story needs to change. This hinge always falls as an outcome of unpredictable events and—in this way—mirrors the unpredictability of life itself.

Narrative logic: A study of the mind of the book's reasoning, narrative logic says not only what we know in the novel but exactly how we have come to know it. Logic has been called the best tool for telling what is true from what is false. This applies to our writing fiction, since writing that seems patently false will fail to interest us.

We depend on two kinds of reasoning in applying logic to our narratives: inductive reasoning, which is evidence offered in the scenes, and then deductive reasoning, which establishes the manner in which these scenes work together.

Narrative pause: A narrative pause is the bridge that often starts a chapter, or a book, in which the narrator is given a broader, more omniscient moment or two to catch up. In doing so, the narraror may speak over the heads of the characters in his tale, say things that these characters cannot know, or establish a sense of the narrative's past or future. It's often constructed in *ambient time* (see entry).

Narrative summary: A scene or action that can be accurately predicted need not be enacted or played out in a scene or episode before the witness of our senses. It can be told in summary because it contains no narrative surprises. The element of surprise is the test of whether or not a scene should be played out. Another word for this is *crisis*.

Narrative territory: Narrative territory is the area in both time and space where a story takes place, defined by temporal mapping.

Narrative weight: A novel is made of elements that have different narrative weights. Scenes that provoke intense feelings in both writer and reader—particularly those scenes containing sex or violent language or action—will feel more dense in terms of their narrative weight than will those scenes in which a character is simply moving along more uneventfully in the direction of conflict.

The novel will exert its own will in terms of tempo. It often understands the rules of narrative in advance of its writer and will ask that a dark scene, which feels heavy, be balanced by one that feels lighter and more effortless. A novel asks that its scenes be varied in terms of its episodes' *internal duration*.

Narrator: The narrator is the voice that tells the story. The term reminds us that it is being told by a person, a storyteller. The novel, therefore, is based in the oral tradition; the words with which it is being told will want to feel as if they could be spoken, not just written.

We are accustomed to having the narrator's point of view shift, for it to attain a global perspective that seems omniscient. Or it can hug up so closely to a certain character that it seems to express that character's thoughts in the very moment they emerge into consciousness.

The narrator takes charge of the storytelling, which is also called the narration. What is seen in the story, and then delegated to the narrator to tell, comes from the noticer. It is the noticer's job to establish the point of view. The noticer, too, may hover in omniscience or hug up close to one character or to several. The noticer may also be centered down inside one character, in which case the narrator assumes this character's voice. His or her story-telling may or may not be reliable but will be necessarily limited to what this character can realistically know.

Noticer: This is the most rudimentary form of point of view, which can be employed to begin a novel by allowing the noticer— either a close third or first person—to enter into the scene in order to witness its events and incidents.

The noticer works as the writer's proxy, by allowing the action of the scene to play out in a haptic way, feeling the hot/cold, wet/dry sense of being in the room where the story's events are spooling forward.

Your noticer is the someone (not the you or the me) who has climbed under the flap of the circus tents and entered into the story. This someone has taken responsibility for finding and occupying the perspective from which the story can best be told. The noticer may be anonymous, as many of us who have ended up writing actually prefer to be, or may be an expert watcher, an overhearer, or eavesdropper. He or she may also be a participant in the story's action, may or may not have a name, may or may not speak in his or her own voice.

Sometimes the noticer seems very closely aligned with the being of the writer—someone who is not the writer per se but who can watch what's going on, hear what's being said, and, where appropriate, think what a character thinks before he has even thought it.

Novel: The novel is a narrative of consequential events involving worthy human characters who change as a result of these events, or else fail to change. (Americans, particularly, may want to insert *tragically* between *else* and *fail*.)

We learn from the study of our solar system that a world will need to be big enough to be round, to be large enough to create its own gravity. This is something a novel—unlike a short story—will want to do.

O

Omniscience: This novelistic all-knowing-ness is tricky and belongs to various forms of agency. Once a novel has been successfully written, we can understand that its "all knowledge" lies in the mind of the book, which encompasses all the ways we have of entering into a scene, via person, point of view, and perspective.

Omniscience is what you and I, in writing these books of ours, arrive at *eventually*. It is probably the novel's own reason for being: its wish to be shown in a way that the meaning of its events and incidents can finally be understood.

Oral nature of the narrative: Sophocles feared that literacy would ruin storytelling by destroying its oral nature. We novelists, well more than two thousand years later, must reassure him that we're worthy inheritors of the story's spoken forms. As your story begins, it is only now learning how to speak. It is, in fact, probably telling itself so that it can learn to tell itself, which it will only understand as it overhears itself.

A story is also telling itself in order to identify its teller. Another name for this is its *narrator*. Every word in your novel will belong to someone. This someone will be—*eventually*, if not exactly now—identifiable.

Identifying your story's narrator determines its narrative stance, which is determined by such technical matters as perspective and point of view. Another name for this is your story's *noticer*. Each book asks to be written by an entirely different noticer, the person who witnessed these events and incidents and lived to tell the tale.

Our task is to help this noticer get the story down, translating from an oral medium into one that is written down. The story is told by the storyteller aloud to be heard by the imagined listener, the writer, who is transcribing the story hurriedly.

It may take awhile to hear the voice of your story's narrator. You may need to write your story in the wrong voice first, so you can find the right one. It may take an entire draft for the storyteller to find the words with which to say what it needs to say. A story wants a manner of talking that adjusts the distance between the teller and the listener. This manner and mode of talking belongs to the story's narrator much more than it belongs to you.

This voice will want to tell the story in a certain way, which is determined by a technical matter linguists call *accommodation*.

Accommodation determines such matters as vocabulary, word choice, and level of diction. It may want to be told in a familiar way, so that the narrator speaks in a manner we might think of a colloquial. Or it may want to sound formal and aloof. These elements are decided as much in the story's unconscious as they are by the writer who sits down to plot them. When is this story being told, for instance, and by whom? To whom does this narrator imagine he or she is speaking? What can we assume that our listeners will understand—and what must be explained?

But the story came first, followed only much later by the clinical terms that name its parts and say why it works. Your story already knows the answers to every question and has come by these answers intuitively. All it wants to do is to begin to speak, which is how it will establish its bonds of intimacy.

P

Parallax, narrative: We rely upon haptic cues to convince us of any scene's reality. In fact, any object—any human being— who is transported out of the realm of the actual undergoes an alteration because of narrative parallax. This results in the fictionalizing that attends the narrative creation—when transported, we become what we are but so much more so. We are reinvented by the essential narrative components and demands of plot and story.

This means that the character "Jane Vandenburgh," displaying my own name—whose dates and life events are *exactly* the same as mine in the longer narrative that I've just published as a memoir—is, nonetheless, *not me*. Narrative parallax freezes an individual as a narrative creation who exists only within the temporal unity of that particular book's time and place.

Perfection in plot or character: Perfection will interest neither the writer nor the reader. We all identify better with characters who are somehow out of balance and therefore on their way somewhere, moving as they must in the direction of whatever is missing, toward what they seek. Whatever is missing, this lack of perfection, makes this character or action feel like life to us.

A plot may be so beautifully constructed that its events telegraph perfection, which will make its resolution predictable, stagnant, and outside human interest.

Plot might be said to be the beautiful edifice your story will inhabit after this story has been given the chance to come to life. Plot *derives* from story, and this develops automatically. Plot *happens* organically in the same way the conch elaborates upon itself to make itself perfectly fit the living shell.

Performance capture: Creating the characters in action can be said to "capture" them in a kind of performance. This turns movement and emotional gesture into the cues that can be read by the senses and sent to the brain for instant translation.

Physicality of words, sound of words on the page: Shirley Jackson says, "Remember, too, that words on a page have several dimensions: they are seen, they are partially heard, particularly if they seem to suggest a sound, and they have a kind of tangible quality—think of the depressing sight of a whole great paragraph ahead of you, solidly black with huge heavy-sounding words."

Moreover, some words seem soft and some hard, some liquid, some warm, some cold. Readers will respond to soft laughter more than to striped laughter or sweet laughter because they can hear "soft" more easily. Itchy and greasy promote a sensual response; scratchy, something rough or smooth.

Plot versus Story: Plot, as Aristotle tells us in his *Poetics*, can best be thought of as an arrangement of the story's incidents and events. These incidents and events are told in episodes of living narrative time that demonstrate their own elements of causation.

This is the Story: The queen died. The king died. Two discrete events whose relationship we don't yet understand. *The queen died, then the king died of grief* describes the sequencing and cause-and-effect relationship between the events of the story. Story powers the rushing current; plot marks its banks.

Plot is the first principle, and we must always make our characters the plot's subordinates. Plot wants to conceal what Story simply goes ahead to show. Plot worries about surprise, also the bigger picture. Plot lies in wait for Story. Plot concerns itself with the theoretical. Plot has in its bag of the tricks all the ways we manipulate narrative time: flashback, flash-forward, exposition, digression, backstory, narrative pauses, and bridges and ellipses.

Plot's paradox: There are two pieces to any plot—say, good versus evil, or a character's moving from ignorance to knowledge—and they are always poised in opposition. Examine any good plot, and you can always find such forces, and the story aims to work them out. We call this plot's paradox because this effort follows the arc of the narrative in a winching action. This shortens moments between actions (with rests), and as the plot unravels, the tension built into the story must necessarily increase.

The plot works always through the tension built of conflict: the notion that change is inevitable, yet human nature resists change. Plot's oppositional forces work always to tie, then untie, the knowledge of *complication*, working in the direction of clarity.

Complication, conflict, and change furnish a plot with the energy it needs to move upward toward the place where it meets its final *crisis*. It is here that the direction of the story changes and its tempo picks up, as it engages in its own *denouement*, or falling action.

A plot—as more and more is known—therefore becomes increasingly mysterious through the process of its unraveling.

Plotline: The plotline is ordered in a manner similar to that of the storyline. With the plotline, however, events are taken out of chronological order to demonstrate cause-and-effect relationships. A scene that happens long ago in the story might be moved along the line of the plot. We could place it, for instance, at the story's apex, since it results in our understanding of all that has happened since.

Plumb line, or true: The novel, whose most basic desire is to have an asymmetrical (balanced in imbalance) symmetry, will want to hang somewhere off the idea of what is "true," which is the human perception of reality. It hangs from the plumb line, a term we import from architecture.

Point of view: Our need for immediacy necessitates that a scene be told from within the room of time where its actions are taking place. The vantage is called perspective or point of view. An omniscient point of view can offer a wide vista, one that then narrows into the intimacy of the close third-person.

Point of view belongs to scene, the story very naturally directing which type it would like the storyteller to use.

Possibility: The writing of stories gave Stephen King what he called "an immense feeling of *possibility* . . . as if [he] had been ushered into a vast building filled with closed doors and had been given leave to open any of them [he] liked."

Provisional draft: The provisional draft—what Anne Lamott calls the Shitty First Draft, or SFD—is written with all the speed a writer can muster. It asks to be the loosest of narratives: scenes written in any order, lines of dialogue written out of context, gestures and descriptions sketched instead of laboriously rendered.

Your SFD will, oddly enough, also contain some remarkably fresh and resonant writing, which is what the storyteller naturally achieves when he or she isn't trying.

Most of the draft will have to be moved, changed, altered for continuity, rewritten time and time again. But a provisional draft of a novel allows it to claim a certain amount of narrative territory. You should feel free to write as broadly and cartoon-ishly as you need to get it down as quickly as you can.

Profanity: The American language is rich with all levels of profan-ity. We theoretically enjoy freedom of speech, but speech acts—including the use of language that others might find vulgar or obscene—have been sanctioned for as long as this wild place of ours has struggled to become a coherent nation.

Indeed, you will be needing *all kinds of* language in your work as a novelist. You will quickly find that what is or is not obscene depends almost entirely upon narrative context.

Fuck was once a societally acceptable word bluntly used to describe an everyday bodily function. This was in Shakespeare's day: Then along came the Puritans, who took issue with the ani-mal functions of the human body.

The Federal Communications Commission is an inheritor of our Puritan heritage and concerns. The FCC sanctions language that reminds us that we seem to possess physical bodies, with this awful, embarrassing propensity to be something aside from pure mind and soul.

As novelists, we really need the sense that our characters are physical beings. We need their senses, as this gives the reader the feeling that he or she can also inhabit the novel's physical place.

And the fact that you and I have physical bodies that cannot live forever is what gives our stories one important part of their meaning, in that we find the life-and-death nature of narrative significance only by becoming keenly aware of our own mortality.

One of the most beautiful books I've ever read takes rank and base mortality as both its theme and subject. *Being Dead*, by Jim Crace, follows the course of a seven-day period wherein the bodies of a married couple, who have been murdered just after they've made love, molder where they lay undiscovered in the dunes. The point of view is lovingly detailed, both omniscient and on the level of the truth accorded to molecular biology, in that we're told what happens on the level of the sand fly, on the level of the dying cell.

Foul language is simply *always* determined by societal context. What we might today consider expletives have derived from the power found in blasphemy. For instance, God's name, except in prayer, wasn't sanctioned, so you'd say *Zounds!* to avoid saying *God's wounds*.

Powerful language can easily overwhelm its narrative context. This is because profanity and blasphemy work in the same primitive, imagistic parts of the mind where we revert in states of dreaming or praying or writing. Our minds, in this way, will freely demonstrate their own primitive belief in word magic. We say *the F word* instead of *fuck* because the latter contains powerful magic, as we once said *Zounds!* to sidestep the image of Jesus, crucified, dying, and bleeding.

The most mild of oaths, *My word!*, is another way of not saying *that* word, the very powerful word a person was never supposed to say: *dog* spelled backward.

Profluence: The novelist John Gardner used the word to describe our falling into the narrative dream. It comes from the Latin for "current" or "flow," and it captures the progression of events caught up in the flow of time.

I have also always taken it to mean *flow* in the way brain scientists and psychologists use the term. They speak of the state in which we are completely lost to the present moment, so deeply immersed in our feeling of participation in the active narrative that it seems to be playing out before the witness of our senses.

It is when we fall into this state that we get a sense of the story's own timelessness and experience the rapture of creation.

Prologue: A prologue, which dates in our language from Chaucer, serves as a preface to the story and is therefore not part of the story. Its function is to set the story up, to offer background details and other useful but perhaps superfluous information. It delays the start of the drama, and because it's a delaying tactic, it can be looked at suspiciously, as a dodge.

The writer needs to look very carefully at who is speaking in the prologue to make certain it isn't *really* the author explaining what he or she is going to be saying in a minute or two.

Prophecy and transformation: It is the mind of the book that will finally know all that it will need to say, as if through an act of its own prophecy. This is why we turn the story over to itself, trusting that it can and will, under its own power, transform.

The story knows, for instance, how its characters match. It prophesies how two events, a half century apart, will somehow rhyme or echo—that after one shoe falls in the story, even if we must wait more than fifty years, we will hear the sound of the other one. This is because our stories have number sense, as does any toddler, deducing, *Two Shoes, One Fell, Now We're Waiting for the Other One.*

The plot might be able to describe this. But the story—if left alone—will do the more *powerful* thing, which is let us discover this on its own and always as if this has *never* been known before. A story has built-in organizational tools that spring directly from the wiring of the human mind; they are made from and reflective of our most ancient psyches. This how its incidents call out to one another over a wide expanse of time, in a manner that is innate to them.

Stories all utilize the fictive elements of prophecy, which says, Listen for the Other Shoe, and transformation, which says, Nothing is *really* as it appears.

Stories left alone come up with characters whose lines of dialogue echo. And if your story's any good, it's stubborn and shy and isn't there in the first row sure of the right answer. You have to be quiet around your story. You sometimes have to wait awhile for it to begin to tell itself to you.

Proportions: There is natural pleasure to be found in the classic proportions, which the longer narrative will intuitively follow. It's where we'll find the final crisis, three-fifths to four-fifths of the way along the arc of the story, with the final fifth being given over to the story's resolution.

The beauty in the rule of fifths was first observed by the philosopher Pythagoras, who first noted the spiritual calm to be found in harmonious numbers. A novel is always a spiritual venture, whereby imbalance of crisis is ultimately resolved in favor of peace, when the story reaches it natural end.

Q

Quest: This derives from an old word that came into English from the French, meaning *hunt*—back in the days when hunting was a high art of great pomp. Our novels have this sense of their task's decorousness, that they are large and complicated affairs with a lineage and history. They should be undertaken with a sense of *mission*.

R

Ranking: The relative placement of an episode or event in a plot will give subliminal cues about its importance. Generally, we remember best those events or incidents that happen *first* or happen *last*. Plot's ability to rank in a series can be used to adjust the seeming importance of its events: The middle of a cardinal sequence, for example, can offer disguise.

Reading (when you're a writer): It's impossible to become a writer of any kind of seriousness unless you read well and deeply in the genre in which you hope to write. If you aren't reading in the genre in which you hope to write, you miss being part of what is actually a complex and interesting conversation.

When I was in school, a writing teacher told us he expected us to treat what we were doing—we were writing fiction—as our religion. In fact, he expected us to tithe: We were told to devote 10 percent of our income to *buying*, actually *paying for*, books written by the kind of writers we hoped to become.

"What?" we asked. "We're poor; we're starving; we're working our way through school."

"I don't care," he said. This is as important as a *spiritual act*.

And so it was that I became a purchaser of books while working as a ticket taker and popcorn maker in a theater that showed what were called *films* instead of *movies*. I bought books when I couldn't afford to buy a coat.

We need to buy books because we need to feel ourselves to be part of this important conversation that stretches from you and me backward to The Ancients and forward to the storytellers still to come.

Here is the great singer-songwriter Judy Collins, on her habit of going to liturgical mass, at home in New York and when she's away, traveling for concerts, of which she gives more than a hundred each year.

"I go to . . . evensong at churches . . . with a choir and liturgy and prayer. I don't sing—I am listening, which is the other side of performing and I get a lot of nurturing from that music . . . that transformative experience of hearing these great choirs," reminding us that we listen from both sides of the page.

Reality: A story's goals remain well hidden because of its inherent need for mystery. So, too, the narrative needs to disguise its own structural mechanics to be taken as believable. Every story in every genre—including science fiction and fantasy—will want to be considered *lifelike*. It will want to be read in the visual cortex of the brain as real by the same mechanisms that make a dream seem real.

It is only by seeming *real* that a story can feel *true*.

Realization: A realization is a thought action that takes on the property of spiritual revelation. We witness a character in the process of changing, in that he or she now understands something that was not understood before.

This character has arrived in a new place, wherein he has a new way of thinking. This is one of the ways our characters' thoughts can earn their way into the narrative, in that their simply *pondering*, or *thinking over this or that*, or *musing* on some subject doesn't interest the twenty-first-century reader.

Consciousness, therefore, must be actively engaged by the novel's plot and its dilemmas for a character to earn the right to think whatever he is thinking. We always look at narrative memories carefully to see how our character's remembering something works to advance the story.

To realize: This is an architectural term meaning "to finally get a project built." The visionary Dutch architect Rem Koolhaas—who calls a building "a volume with skin"—asked Milanese architect Giancarlo de Carlo: "How many of your buildings have been realized?" "Not many," de Carlo said, "maybe 15 percent." "Better than me," Koolhaas said. "For me it's more like 10." De Carlo smiled, "Only 10 for me too."

And it may be that we novelists will realize about 10 percent of the books that we fall asleep conceiving. So what?

Recognition: The elements of plot are revealed to the writer largely by the process of *actually writing* the story. So the element of *recognition* appears of its own accord as a character, for instance, says something the writer didn't realize the character knew. This reinforces the sense that the characters are real and live apart from the writer's imagination. Recognition is that moment when the writer looks at a character in action or hears him or her speak, and thinks, *That's right; I know that about you.*

Resolution: Every crisis works in the direction of its own resolution. There are two kinds of resolutions available to us as writers of the longer narrative. One is temporary and unstable; the other is permanent, fixed.

We identify the type of resolution according to where it lies along the narrative arc. If it happens early in the story, we understand it to be hollow. It cannot *really* resolve the crisis, so it will almost immediately open out into a new series of complications and plot-laden entanglements.

This is true of every crisis that resolves *before* the apex of the triangular rise. Its resolution will be *temporary* and will contribute to another conflict. We also will not believe in it as a true resolution.

If the resolution happens after the final crisis, it will be permanent or *true*. It will contribute to the sense that all mysteries are being solved and the lost status quo is being carefully reinstated.

Periodic resolutions of crises allow the action to pause and regroup before it swings back into flight like the circus performer poised at the top of a stanchion high in the tent right before he leaps. Suspense asks that we don't really know whether these temporary resolutions are true or false.

The upward arc says this story is actively moving away from stability. It is moving *onward*, because change is essential to a story, so it always pursues risk. The narrative positioned along an upward slope is angled in the direction of the unknown, pointing toward the danger that is found in the unpredictable. The narrative moves always in the direction of the part of the future that cannot be foretold.

Reversal: A story can turn so that a situation may be reversed. We can move from a state of knowing into one of unknowing, or from unknowing to understanding. These reversals are the most powerful elements of suspense, wherein good can be seen to triumph over evil, or evil over good.

Every reversal must adhere, however, to our sense of what is probable and what might *actually* and realistically occur given the story's inherent narrative logic.

Rising action: The upward slope of the story is its rising action. The feeling of ascendancy is crucial to the longer narrative; our interest can be sustained for only as long as we feel headed into a narrative's future, into conflict. We need to feel the story to be progressing, to be headed deeper into its own mysteries, that it's getting somewhere. We want always to have the sense that there'll be more high-wire tricks ahead, that there's a death-defying reason for us to be paying this story such close attention.

It's by *rising action* that a story achieves its sense of mystery and anticipation, both of which are crucial to the longer narrative. Each conflict must be experienced as *meaningful*, building upon one another toward the final crisis. This will be resolved as the novel's various storylines meet to solve themselves.

Risk: For us to apprehend a story as lifelike, characters must enter into situations that place them *at risk*. A feeling of risk—that we are moving into an unknown and unknowable future—is the third rail of the upward arc of the narrative, by which the story is given the power to continue.

If a story has gone flat, it's almost always because the element of risk is not apparent.

S

Scene: In working out the elements of plot, the writer must place the action of the story before the eyes of the audience. A scene, once written as a temporal episode, becomes a solid element. It can then be studied and moved along the arc of the story, to wherever it offers the most suspense and significance.

Whenever you get lost—and most of us get lost a thousand times over the course of writing and rewriting a novel—you can settle yourself back in along the storyline by writing a scene. Your story always has another scene ready it would like to show to you.

Scene vs. summary of scene: Showing an action is all that a story is, since it comprises its events and incidents. The only way to get at these events and incidents is by the witness of our senses in scene: seeing and hearing the events, feeling the temperature of the room, smelling the air, tasting the food that's being eaten.

Summarizing what went on in a scene, meanwhile, is the plot recounting what's occurred according to *somebody's point of view.* This summary leaves out details and is open to misinterpretation. A summary proves that there are myriad versions of our one same tale, that there is no truly neutral witness. Point of view and its more-or-less certain reliability belongs to plot, just as scene belongs to story.

Sentence: Narrative began, the linguists tell us, with the ability of human beings to direct one another's gaze by gesture. This, in turn, aids our own ability to see what reality is made of, in that it is actually experienced in a community. The sentence is the first story that any of us tells. Someone did something. Something resulted from this action. All storytelling proceeds from there.

Sequencing: This is the order in which plot enters the rooms of time. The scenes that the story makes are set out in a cause-and-effect relationship that calls for their chronology to be minimized. This allows their associative relationships to emerge. If story says events happen 1, 2, 3, then plot's sequencing will ask that they be arranged first, second, third so we can understand their meaning.

Situation: A story exists within its temporal and geographical context, its place in time and space. The story's situation contributes language to its almost wordless nature. We sense that this rather ancient story is being told this way, this time, using this body of language. The mind of the book holds all these parts in balance, knowing that the story is being told in this specific variation.

Speech: A character speaks whenever moved by a thought act that defines this individual as a piece of the ongoing dramatic narrative. A character should not speak simply to declaim whatever he or she thinks, nor as a means of expressing any supposed "individuality."

Speech takes up room in the narrative; it is a dense material. It also takes time and effort to craft plausibly and at appropriate length. One of the more important reasons to write a first draft is to import into your realm the language you are using to create it. We do this by sitting down and writing out our stories. In this writing out, you will *hear* your characters as they begin to speak.

Language will eventually start to count in a detailed, itsy-bitsy way. We will start to attend to breath pauses and whether someone's line of dialogue needs to be tagged, whether this tag needs to be described so the reader can hear *how* the writer wants this line to be heard.

The time for that, however, is *not* now, not in this early draft. Right now you get to spend and spend in the manner of someone who's just won the lottery, which means you write and write and write, and you don't need to worry at all about its being either good or pretty, or whether the characters know what they're saying before they speak.

Let them speak. Let them say anything they want, as what they say is sure to surprise you.

Sprung triangle: The action as we've described in the entry *abstracted isosceles* rises along an arc, moving as a vector—or an arrow that indicates narrative speed, weight, and force. It moves away from its triangulated base. This is the natural form of the narrative, and we let our stories mess with it.

Storyline: The dream of the narrative follows this flat, fast track, episode by episode, to claim its own territory in time and space. A storyline is defined only by its scenes. These play out in dramatic fashion before the witness of both the writer's and the reader's senses.

The storyline lies horizontally, while the plot rises along the path described by the sprung triangle.

Succumbing to plot: A character must stand up to its own plot—and not be overwhelmed by it—in the same way each of us is asked to stand up and confront the misfortunes in our own lives. When a plot triumphs too completely and easily, our characters suspend their own natures and will feel flattened and altered. They'll be rendered uninteresting because of overwhelming circumstance—reduced, essentially, to victims of this circumstance.

Surprise: We want a surprise to emerge from the plot as a logical extension of cause and effect. We don't want it to seem illogical or sprung upon us, as if too many clowns are popping, unbidden, out of the narrative VW.

Surprise decrees that a character stay in character, that his or her surprising actions plausibly arise from an alteration in circumstance. The circumstance must ask a character to dynamically step into a future that is not predetermined.

Suspense: For reasons of suspense, the narrative must hide its ending off the sightline beyond the turn where the story arrives at C. The crisis to be found at C will lie—and this is rather predictable—somewhere three-fifths to four-fifths along the narrative journey.

Symmetry: Symmetry is an exact correspondence in size or form, or an arrangement of parts to make them match and balance. Because of our pleasure in the golden mean, we prefer for symmetries in a novel to be broken and to be allowed to spiral outward, which prompts our opening the plot to possibility.

Sympathy: One of the three tests that measure whether our characters and/or elements of plot lie within the Modern Realistic Tradition. They must inspire our sympathy, they must inspire our *empathy* (see entry), and their actions must correlate to our intuition about reality.

T

Tactile quality of the written narrative: We enter the written narrative to find the world of story, which should be as enveloping as a dream. We should feel the silk of a loved one's back, the warmth of a loved one's breath. The written narrative has no equal in creating this sense of immediacy and intimacy, in which we learn all we can about another's existence.

Talent: Often a hindrance, talent seems to demand that a writer write well. When you're just getting started with a novel, writing well doesn't matter much at all. Those who understand themselves to be "talented" also like to show off this talent. They also become impatient.

Temporal mapping: The preliminary draft offers the writer an opportunity to map each of the areas, in narrative time and space, that the novel has visited. When I make a temporal map I code its areas thematically so I can see how these are related. I also place them next to one another in various combinations, to see how these might or might not resonate.

Tension: The tension in a plot is maintained by the sense that the narrator has the story entirely in hand. The three pieces of the story are made by uniting *plot* to *fictional time* to the *significance* of the action being seen.

Terror: Writing in action is frightening. Our fear will jolt the writing to life, quickening it by imparting its own sense of risk and meaning.

Our fear of what may happen while writing helps wrench the narrative out of the stillness of the status quo and it is allowed to move in the direction of its own discoveries, which lie in the future.

Narrative action will feel—to writer and reader—like a bodily sensation. We feel as if we're in a carnival ride, belted in and suddenly being *jerked* out of narrative stasis and *forward* into the story's future.

We are now *on our way* whether we really want to be or not. We're going even if we're not entirely sure this ride is safe or will be *good* for us. We're being yanked upward toward the fear and excitement of the unknown, and before you know it, we're *gone*.

As a story's action begins, it is meant to frighten us. Something is going to happen; whatever this something is, is oddly *out of our control*.

Our stories seem to live in us and through us and remain somehow apart from us, in that they are not exactly *products* of everything we've learned and now know. Like our dreams, they stand at a bizarre angle to what feels like our more mundane existence, which is why we're afraid of them.

This fear imparts its own tension, as they grapple with us for narrative control.

The story exists to convince, to be believable. Allowing it to launch itself into its own risky future is part of the necessary danger every narrative faces. Writing in narrative action allows the story to exist outside our careful planning and plotting and our sense of linguistic mastery. Our stories benefit from each and every risk we take. We take a risk when we trust them, when we bravely allow the narrative itself to determine how far and fast it wants to go.

The End: "For the sake of verisimilitude and realism," John O'Hara wrote, "you cannot positively give the impression of an ending: you must let something hang. A cheap interpretation of that would be to say that you must always leave a chance for a sequel."

The more profound reason is that the Ending that ties all elements up perfectly will not be believed. It won't resonate as being *like life*, which posits perfection only to wrest it immediately away in order to break it.

A story wants its own fractal ending, for it to reference its own irregular regularity. The disorder of its nature and the imperfect way it will arrive is its own completion.

Thinking: Whenever a character is allowed to think instead of engage in action, this thinking lies heavily along the line of the story. Often, this isn't being thought by the character at all—it's the author trying to slip in a little background or to work in a little plot development in voice-over. So eventually—not necessary in the first through fifteenth drafts, but eventually—you will check every moment when a character is caught in a moment of thinking. You will make sure that this isn't the writer doing a little *authorial intrusion*, telling the reader what we think the reader needs to know.

A character can, of course, *think*, since this is one of the things human beings actually do. Characters can think as long as this thinking moves the story along the narrative arc, in which case it stops being "thinking" and becomes the "thought act" that brings to the narrative the possibility for change.

Thought act: A thought act allows the narrator to share consciousness with a character. Through it, we can overhear a character's unspoken thoughts at the exact moment these thoughts are emerging into language. Thoughts are important if used carefully and judiciously. A thought act can give us the character in the exact moment that he or she realizes something important. That is: I used to think this, but now (because of the actions of plot and story) I think something different.

These *thought acts* are different in that they have the ability to change the story's narrative direction. A realization is, in fact, one of the more important dramatic *turns* a story can make. It's where we see a character in a moment of very intimate internal *change.*

Threes: Threes are simply more interesting sets than are twos, which tend to want to match and balance. This is why a story works off the *sprung triangle* instead of the more easily divided quadrangle. We find the story's odd harmony in the way its apexes will all be marked with the letter C: for conflict, crisis, change, those same old triangulated consequences.

Time lengths: A novel will quickly establish it own tempo and rhythm—we measure these in narrative time lengths. They clock an episode's ability to triangulate between conflict and resolution of this conflict, before the story moves on in the direction of its next conflict or complication.

A novel's time length, as in a musical signature, will establish the rhythm that will echo and repeat, which the narrative will then use in its patterns and themes. Each is run by its own highly individualized clock. The time lengths of a novel's episodes measure *interior duration.* The clocks of some longer narratives will have its episodes spooling along lazily, while others begin loudly, shockingly, then go on to transpire with rapid-fire staccato.

Each and every episode will echo and repeat the novel's larger sense of narrative tempo.

Tone: The tone of one's writing—whether light, comedic, ironic, somber, simple and straightforward—is one of the kaleidoscopic aspects that work together to make the novel exactly what it wants to be. A change in perspective—the distance or angle or view from which we regard a scene's events—will change the tone of the narrator's storytelling. These events will be seen either more or less intimately.

Tone is simple; it's also, often, difficult, and may be the last thing a writer gets a handle on.

Tracking data: If the narrative is taking place in an actual time/space continuum (as opposed to the mind of the writer), the scene will render tracking data that will need to make sense.

The voice of the narrator inhabits the narrative space at a very specific point in time and gathers information that makes inherent storytelling sense.

This means the point of view in which the story is being told is logical, that the noticer can reasonably see what the story needs for it to see. The narrator, meanwhile, should be up to the job of reporting it, and the storyteller equipped with the maturity and vocabulary to say what needs to be said.

Transience: The form of the novel—its great sweep, its sense of life-and-death consequence—derives from its ability to contain and express the transience of all human endeavor. We die, no matter how beautiful are the things that we think and make. We die no matter how hard we pray. We all die, the novel knows, in a way no other art form as readily and heartbreakingly tells us.

U

Unity: Every good book achieves a sense of artistic unity. Everything necessary to the story is made known with no superfluous element left to lie heavily upon the line of action. This comes from the ancient idea that every part of the whole thematically mirrors the whole.

Unraveling or unfurling of the plot: The character is presented with a dilemma; this dilemma worsens into conflict; conflict worsens into crisis, which demands action, which yields either a favorable or unfavorable outcome—or one whose nature we see but cannot yet apprehend.

V

Vector, or force vector: An entity, possessing both magnitude and direction, that can be represented by an arrow whose width and length is proportional to the magnitude. Its orientation in space represents the direction of the action.

Verisimilitude: It's one of the most basic tests of narrative logic: Does this seem to us to be true? Verisimilitude is the piece of storytelling that appeals to our deductive reasoning. Those of us working in the Modern Realistic Tradition, those of us who want our work to hold up the mirror to life, work to make our novels seem real. We strive to avoid authorial intrusion, to refrain from continually interrupting ourselves, to become invisible enough that the story gains the strength of its own conviction. We do not want to remind ourselves, our readers, or the story itself that it is "only art," as if art were a lesser form of existence.

Art, in the hearts and souls of its true believers (such as the writer of this book) strives to seem *more true than true*. This quality of appearing to be true, of our need to hone toward an art that very carefully depicts reality in a highly organized and systematic way, is one of the chief pleasures of telling and hearing a story.

The more careful the storyteller, the more the story will resemble reality in even its smallest details. Realism and plausibility are especially important ingredients in getting your reader to engage with the story and to believe what you'd like them to believe.

An audience wants to participate in *belief*. It wants to contribute to a *collective* suspension of disbelief. My convincing *you*—and hoping that there are *many of you*—that my story is true also helps to convince *me* of its reality.

Vocation: Writing chooses us, as many novelists will tell you. I no more decided that I would be a novelist than I decided to be born a girl. Writing has this sense of vocation, that we are called to it. This cloistered aspect causes us to be both of the world we're writing about and not exactly participant. It was something Gustave Flaubert viewed as "a monkish vocation requiring the sacrifice of all else." He stayed away from anything he thought might tempt or distract him. And he continued living in his provincial hometown of Croisset with what one of his biographers has called "the illustrious company of the dead [in order] to devote himself to the worship of art."

For most of us, being a novelist needn't be this extreme. Though we absolutely will feel the life that seems to have chosen us is *exactly* this.

W

The way we name a river: I recently came upon a review written by Eudora Welty of the kind of book that is exactly what every beginning novelist needs on her or his shelf: George R. Stewart's *Names on the Land: A Historical Account of Place-Naming in the United States*, published in 1945.

Welty, one of our best writers in the modern American idiom and an insightful guide to how fiction works, noted Stewart's account of how Indian words have come into the American language: by transference, translations, or false etymology. Welty wrote:

The Indian names [that endure] are of course not the actual, original Indian names . . . [rather] they are what the French priests wrote down, what the Spanish thought [a word] sounded like, what the English [imagined these Indians] undoubtedly meant, what the Dutch made sound as nearly Dutch as they could [by adding a "kill" to its end]. Schenectady, for instance, is an anglicized form of the Dutch conception of an . . . Indian word.

The Dutch brought the sound of the Indian word into the language, while the English would try to translate the word for meaning. This brings us to a major difference in the way a Native American or a white person would name a river, as Stewart points out. The European concept of a river was of that one entire system, a stream with all its sources back to its headwaters, all of its tributaries mapped and traced.

"What is the name of this river?" white explorers would ask a Native American.

"Big Rock," the Native American would say, meaning this to be the name of the river *exactly there*.

A little way downstream, this same river would be named Little Bend.

Mississippi is a French version of an Algonquin word, which may (or may not) have originally meant "big river." It could have never meant "Father of the Waters," as many of us were taught in school, since this is not the way an Indian would *ever* name a river.

In order to write our scenes, we go to a specific place in the story, which can be any place at all. We accurately name the river *there* by describing its action as carefully as possible. We don't worry at all about its tributaries or headwaters or where the river (which is our story) is going to spill into the sea.

We write one piece of the river and call it Big Rock, then we write the one called Little Bend.

We enter the time of our story and look around. It may seem as wild and as strange as the New World did to the first European explorers. We look around, entering it respectfully, listening to the voice of those who already live there to find out what the story's things want to call themselves.

We enter our story as we would a foreign country.

Witness: The reader needs a conduit for entering the narrative space. This happens via the function of the witness, which is the present-tense sense of becoming personally, physically present and involved in the story's reality. It is the feeling of being pulled in, that you are able to see what the scene holds for you, to feel its own knowledge and hear what it needs to say.

Work: This is work. Writing a novel is hard, hard work. You will lose faith in the work completely. It will seem to get worse the more effort you put into it.

We call it "a work" for this reason. It doesn't just *happen*: It is something we toil long and hard in order to create. The effort feels more stubborn than artistic. It calls on us to become well acquainted with our most base and abject selves. We have no idea, most of the time, why we've started out doing this, no idea what might come of it, except that it can never be worth all the tens of thousands of hours of labor.

The work is thankless. No one needs it. There will be no monetary recompense. No one rational would actually *choose this*, we will think not once or twice but over and over again.

The point is, we *all feel this way; we all also feel this way almost all the time.*

Worldview: The writer of the longer narrative is ambitious and has set out to create not only a world but a worldview. In creating a world we fill the narrative space with time and energy and matter. It also says what is and is not important, what holds people together, what drives them apart. Something fills the air of this place we are making that has never before existed.

In the novels I see in progress, what fills the air for me is this great sense of the larger American enterprise, that smart people are out there doing what they do.

Our characters grow up and learn to speak and begin to fill the air with the majesty of what seems like their perfect animal being, just as you and I—in making the worlds we do—fill the air with language that is equally invented and wishful.

I think of something my daughter recently said about how I so readily misquote her in both fiction and the nonfiction I write and in the stories I tell into the air of my real life.

"It's not what I said," Eva told me. "It's what you *wish* I'd said."

Y

Your story's needs: Though the needs of a story are simple, it isn't easy to remember this. We start writing and almost immediately want to try to write well. We also want to write individualistically; we want to write with style.

This is why: We've read all these good books, have read many more good books than we'll ever have a chance to write. So instead of doing the more simple thing that is actually called for as we start out—which is writing our story's incidents and events in whatever order they occur to us—we begin to write in a manner we believe will demonstrate that we write well.

Writing well is one of the least reliable predictors of your being able to write a novel. If anything, writing well probably hurts your chance. Those of us who write well—I write well, I also write really easily, neither of which has ever helped me—are often vexed by our own good writing. That's because it so often sounds disturbingly *off*, as if it's listening to itself as it goes about being good writing.

It's simply *not important* that any of us writes well as a story's getting itself ready to tell itself to us. Trying to write well, in fact, gets in the way of the harder thing, which is allowing the story to tell itself honestly.

It's trying to tell itself simply and honestly, as we're trying to *listen* to the story, trying to get it down.

We need to remember to listen to our story. A story exists as an oral medium in the storyteller's mind, and it isn't yet rendered in its written form. This is the simple task you and I are charged with doing. What we are is our story's scribe.

A story stays alive as long as it isn't written down—the trick for you and me is to render it on the page in a manner that *feels* like it is just as lively as when it is told to us.

Writing, in fact, is secondary to the fact of the narrative's existence. We write only as a corollary to the storytelling event.

We write, in fact, in order to feel ourselves in the presence of this magnificent force, that even here, even now, as we only begin to listen, will start to well up in us.

RECOMMENDED READING

WRITERS READ. NOVELISTS read other novelists. We do best when we read those writers who seem to be glancing over the heads of everyone else to speak directly to us. To find your own best teachers you find those writing the greatest books in the genre in which you work. These are the books you wish you'd written.

We tend to look to the experts only when we feel stuck. The following books on writing and the craft of fiction have been invaluable to me in my thinking about what's gone wrong:

Bird by Bird: Some Instructions on Writing and Life, by Anne Lamott, has invaluable tips that help writers at all levels get going and keep going.

How Fiction Works, by James Wood, introduced me to the concept of "the noticer," so useful to our discussions of person, perspective, and point of view. Wood has also nailed why an *authorial intrusion* works to ruin the narrative dream by outlining the three kinds of writing that do belong on the page.

The word *profluence* in my usage comes from John Gardner, used in his several fine books on writing.

I reread E. M. Forster's wonderful *Aspects of the Novel* every time I prep to teach a workshop in the longer narrative, as no one else has a sweeter, more encouraging tone.

I am indebted to Eudora Welty for her eloquent discussion of narrative time in *The Eye of the Story*, which changed my own perceptions, even as the discovery of her humorous, smart, and distinctively American voice once encouraged me believe that I, too, could become a writer. I saw her once riding down to the lobby in an elevator in the Algonquin in New York. I didn't speak to her, not wanting to intrude, but it seemed to me we did twinkle in one another's direction.

I always listen particularly carefully when visual artists talk about their work, as it's so helpful in thinking about how a narrative of any size must remember its own sense of material substance. In this regard, I'm particularly indebted to Francis D. K. Ching, whose clear and beautiful drawings from his *A Visual Dictionary of Architecture* have so inspired me.

I also read and reread Aristotle's *Poetics*, as it continually serves to remind me that we're working in a lineage that is both deep and old, one where everything is only as complicated as it is simple, and that there is really actually so little new under the sun.

ACKNOWLEDGMENTS

I T MAY BE that there are two kinds of writers in the world: those who know what they're going to say and who sit down and say it. They are called the writers of expository prose—a thousand thousand times over the years it's taken me to write this book, I've wished I was one of them.

Then there are those of us who set out with what we hope are clear instructions on where we think we're going, only to find ourselves spectacularly lost. We are the storytellers.

Because I am a storyteller by nature, nurture, breeding, and inclination, the writing of this book of expository prose—the how-to book on how to tell a story—has been one of the hardest projects I've ever undertaken.

It has been, therefore, my amazing good fortune to have had the help of a team put together by Counterpoint, that writer's dream of a publishing house: Laura Mazer, who freely confessed she had only the faintest notion of what I *might be* getting at, but continued to believe it was worth exploring, and Bob Ickes, who has taken the Shaker approach to building this book, making it simpler to make it sound, and has literally saved this book by giving it, and me, the concept of the topic sentence. Counterpoint's great staff includes Roxy Aliaga and April Wolfe, who've been of special help in making this the book it is.

And encouraging me to start, encouraging me to keep going, encouraging me to finish have been my most staunch supporters, Trish Hoard and Jack Shoemaker, who don't put up with quitters. I'm enormously grateful to my novel-writing students who've looked at parts of this over the years and have offered suggestions, including Susan Badger-Jones, Tiffany Fuchs, Rita Gardner, Charlie Haas, Autumn Harrison, Irene Isley, B. K. Moran, Janice Newton, Kerry Radcliffe, Pam Steele, and Hillary Wiley.

I am forever indebted to Fishtrap, the writers' community in Wallowa County in eastern Oregon, for the opportunity to teach the yearlong novel-writing workshop, and, in particular, to Rich Wandschneider, Rick Bombaci, and Janis Carper.

This is dedicated to the storytellers, all those who've been our guides as we've wandered in the wilderness, as well as all of those still to come, and to the memory of Ross Feld, Gus Blaisdell, Gina

Berriault, and Guy Davenport, who've gone on to walk the star path but whose stories are with us still.